T5-DGJ-604

GOD'S

PLAN

FOR

YOUR

LIFE

LIBRARY
LINCOLN MEMORIAL UNIVERSITY
Harrogate, Tennessee 37752

230908

DAVID D. SULLIVAN

BX6154 .S84 1993
Sullivan, David D.
God's plan for your life.

Copyright © 1993 by David D. Sullivan
All rights reserved.

Printed in U.S.A.

Cover design by Tami Faudi, and computer-drawn by
Kathleen Pauner, using CorelDRAW.
Diagrams by Todd Jordan.

Unless otherwise indicated, Scripture quotations in this
book are taken from THE HOLY BIBLE,
NEW INTERNATIONAL VERSION. Copyright 1973,
1978, 1984 International Bible Society. Used by permission
of Zondervan Bible Publishers.

Scripture quotations marked *NKJV* are taken from the *New
King James Version*, Holy Bible. Copyright 1979, 1980, 1982
by Thomas Nelson Inc., Publishers. Used by permission.

Scripture quotations marked KJV are taken from the King
James Version.

All italicized and upper-case words in this book are of the
author's emphasis.

Library of Congress Catalog Card Number 93-92767

ISBN 0-9637295-1-9

LIBRARY OF CONGRESS

OCT 27 1993

COPYRIGHT OFFICE

C

Dedicated to

My father, Hugh D. Sullivan,
in the hope that he will say yes
to the One who loves him,
and will not let him go.

LIBRARY OF CONGRESS

OCT 27 1993

COPYRIGHT OFFICE

CONTENTS

1.	The Currency of Heaven	9
2.	God Found Guilty	15
3.	Why Running Doesn't Work	21
4.	The Christ Who Cries with You	31
5.	How to Be Born	39
6.	How to Walk	51
7.	A Lesson from Gorillas	63
8.	A Plan in Search of a Person	73
9.	The Taste Test	81
10.	Defended by the Judge	85
11.	What's in a Day?	101
12.	America's Changing Face	125
13.	Old Lies in a New Age	131
14.	The Right Attitude	139
15.	Stepping out in Faith	145

Acknowledgments

To Carl Coffman, Richard Davidson, Maxine Nicola, and Russ Potter for their critical reading of the manuscript and helpful input.

To Kathleen Pauner for painstakingly typesetting the manuscript in Ventura Publisher, and skillfully working with the cover illustration. You are an unusually kind and caring soul.

To Tami Faudi for her creative cover illustration. Your labyrinth leads one to the Author of life.

To the Evangelist Lyle Pollett for his winning ways, and for his chair illustration. I've learned to truly sit.

To Jerry Bowers for his cogent insights on the "woman at the well."

To the hundreds of people around the country who have agreed to pray daily for those who read this book.

To my sweet wife Susana for her love, and for her support of this project. Thank you for being a patient, honest sounding-block.

To my dear children Briana and Elijah, for the joy they have brought me, and the patience they have taught me. May you always walk with the Lord.

To my courageous mother Joyce for her prayers, and for her commitment to life, when life is most harsh. Don't look back.

To my Lord Jesus Christ, for finding me when I was lost, washing me when I was filthy, and strengthening me when I was weak. You are an awesome Savior! Thank you for putting up with my rebelliousness, and thank you for filling my life with purpose. May your Spirit lovingly reach out to the reader through every page of this book.

Chapter 1

THE CURRENCY OF HEAVEN

Not long ago I applied for and received a loan to help relieve our financial situation. While much of that sum of money was already accounted for and earmarked for specific tasks, somehow there was still a little of it left over—about $600.

Immediately my mind began to meander through its playground of wishful thinking. Various items appeared here and there that I had long hoped to acquire, but never could. It was a lot of fun actually—an extremely rare but pleasing problem for my wife and I. Just how should this remaining money be used.

I found myself inwardly asking the question, "If God had $600, how would He spend it?" It was a fleeting moment of sincere childlikeness in a world which forces all of us to grow up much too quickly.

His opinion and example were important to me. It was an honest question, and real too. My own response came just as quickly. "God doesn't deal with money in heaven. It's a different realm."

So if God does not use our kind of currency up there, what currency does He use? (1) With *what* does He buy things? (2) Furthermore, *what does He buy?* (3) And thirdly, *why* would He buy something anyway?

These questions are answered in reverse order in John
3:16:

(3) "For God so *loved* . . ."

(2) "the *world* . . ."

(1) "that He gave His one and only *Son*, that whoever
believes in Him shall not perish but have eternal life."

To secure your salvation, God spent His most treasured possession on you: Jesus Christ, His beloved Son.
That says a lot about God, a lot about you, and a lot
about His Son. But we'll get into that later.

When God spent Jesus on you, it was no ordinary
transaction. The Bible says in 1 John 3:1, "How great is
the love the Father has *lavished* on us, that we should be
called children of God!"

It makes a person feel valuable and loved when he is
treated extravagantly. For the apostle John it was a matter
of re-emphasizing what he had experienced first-hand:
the *giving*, the *lavishing* of Jesus Christ upon the human
race. You are a vital part of that race. You are a member *of*
it, and a runner *in* it. Let the beauty of the fact sink in:
Jesus has been given for *you*.

A Sound Investment

Economically, heaven is quite stable, when you understand what Currency it is based on. And God is as efficient a Manager as He is a Creator. He is thorough in His
work, calling it "good" after He accomplishes something.
He invests wisely too. Instead of investing in junk bonds or
other "things," as we might, He chooses to invest in *people*,
because "things" are temporal; but people can be *eternal*.

Viewing yourself as an investment will radically influence how you live your life. It does wonders for your self-concept, and gives abundant meaning to an otherwise meaningless existence.

You need not spend a dime, for the program is free, and best of all—its origin is *outside* of you, not within you. That's good news because you might not always feel too good about yourself.

Many books and seminars nowadays focus on the personal power inside of you that must be tapped, in order to exert an influence over your life. Well, God's plan is quite different.

Our Predicament

His program takes into consideration the human condition. It is an honest, realistic evaluation, and deserves our attention. For all of the incredible accomplishments of humankind, we have never been able to do anything about the human heart.

The Bible says in Jeremiah 17:9, "the heart is deceitful above all things and beyond cure. Who can understand it?" Speaking of man, Genesis 8:21 says, "every inclination of his heart is evil from childhood." Jesus said, in Matthew 15:19, "for out of the heart come evil thoughts, murder, adultery, sexual immorality, theft, false testimony, slander." And just in case we might begin to think we are exempt from this condition, God adds these words: "*All* have turned aside, they have together become corrupt; there is no one who does good, not even one" (Psalm 14:3). "For *all* have sinned and fall short of the glory of God" (Romans 3:23).

The accuracy of God's evaluation is attested to by the fact that even the very best and brightest people have done terrible things. The universality of sin is evident everywhere— all one has to do is pick up the local newspaper. The media thrive on sensationalistic sin, because people thrive on it. We actually *enjoy* sin, which is why it is so popular.

That is how desperately wicked we are. We enjoy the things that kill us. And the "sins" we do are simply manifestations or outworkings of the "SIN" that we ARE. We have all inherited a sinful human nature, and so we don't even have to be tempted to do evil. We'll get into it just fine if left to ourselves. This is precisely why Jesus said He wanted to set up camp in the individual human heart. "The kingdom of God is *within* you." "You should not be surprised at my saying, 'You must be born again'" (Luke 17:21; John 3:7).

Can You Be Bought?

Jesus is the Currency of Heaven, and you are the soul who has been "bought." Actually, the Bible uses words like "redeem" and "ransom." They express the idea of someone or something being purchased, atoned for, or rescued from an adverse situation.

One of the many features that attract me to God is that although He is frank and up front with us about our sin, He also shares the *good* news in the same breath:

The Situation		The Good News
"Though your sins are like scarlet,"	⟶	"they shall be as white as snow" (Isaiah 1:18).
"For all have sinned and fall short of the glory of God,"	⟶	"and are justified freely by His grace through the redemption

that came by Christ Jesus"
(Romans 3:23, 24).

"For the wages of sin   ⟶   "but the gift of God is eternal life
is death,"   in Christ Jesus our Lord"
                              (Romans 6:23).

To be sure, our redemption was not *free* even though it was freely given. It cost God something. Rather, it cost Him the death of some*one*—His dear Son—His *only* Son.

In one sense, you have already been redeemed. On the other hand, you can never be redeemed until you choose to be. This contrast between God's desire for you and your own ability to accept or reject Him is the reason for the writing of this book. I simply wish to make the salvation matter clear, and to paint a picture of Jesus that is utterly irresistible.

His Motive

Why is God so interested in you? Perhaps He sees something you have missed. You and I can *talk* about love; we can experience it and exhibit it towards just about anything or anyone, if we so desire. But here we see a major difference between us and God.

"God IS love" (1 John 4:8). Love is something He IS, not merely what He does or how He feels. Therefore, He cannot help but love. Love is the primary motive for everything God does. "For God so *loved*" (this is His springboard for action) "that He *gave*" (and this is His action).

Even in His judgments God's motive is love. He knows that some people would never be happy being with Him for eternity, so He doesn't force them to be. But

He tries vigorously to win our love and allegiance. We'll probably never realize all the many avenues He has used to reach us.

Chapter 2

GOD FOUND GUILTY

I remember watching a talk-show on TV, where the guest was a young man who several years earlier had murdered his parents. He had felt so much anger towards them, and wasn't able to deal with it. He planned out exactly how he was going to do it, leaving no detail ignored. He even rehearsed his ghastly plot the night before his parents were to return home from a weekend trip.

When that dreadful Sunday night arrived he waited—crouching in the bushes for two hours. When his parents pulled into the driveway he carried out his wicked scheme. It was pure, unadulterated, premeditated murder in the first degree.

The Forethought of You

Before the earth was made or the human race created, God the Father, God the Son, and God the Holy Spirit got together in a "spiritual huddle" or "salvific caucus," if you will. The three of them discussed the glorious prospect of a race of beings created in their image and called by their name.

This race would naturally be given the freedom to trust God and walk with Him, or to choose a different leader. It was agreed that if something was to go wrong and these

humans actually chose *against* God, Jesus—the Son—
would lay down His life so that the fallen race could be
saved.

Before "sin" came into existence Christ already had a
Savior mindset. He is "the Lamb that was slain from the
creation of the world" (Revelation 13:8), even though His
actual death on Golgotha's cross would take place some
4,000 years in the future. He was ready and willing to
follow through if the race should fall into sin. And that's
exactly what we did.

Salvation, then, was a FORETHOUGHT, not an after-
thought. You were thought of and loved long before you
were born. You were on Christ's mind in that huddle and
you were on His mind when He bled upon the cross. You
are *still* on His mind. It will always be that way. Nothing
you can do or say—however wicked—can change that.

To be sure, God was aware of the risks involved in His
plan. He knew. He even understood the outcome, and yet
He still went ahead with it. He knew that a good number
of us would misunderstand His purpose and motive. He
knew that many would mistake Him for His arch-enemy.
He even knew that a majority would reject His plan. But
the plan must go on.

Premeditated Salvation

Listen to what the apostle Paul has to say about God's
plan: "He [God] CHOSE us in him [Christ] BEFORE the
creation of the world to be holy and blameless in his sight.
In love he predestined us to be ADOPTED as his sons
through Jesus Christ, in accordance with his PLEASURE
and will—to the praise of his glorious GRACE, which he
has freely given us in the One he loves. In him [Christ]

we have redemption through his blood, the forgiveness of sins, in accordance with the riches of God's grace that he LAVISHED on us with all WISDOM and UNDER-STANDING. And he made known to us the MYSTERY of his will according to his good pleasure, which he purposed IN CHRIST, to be put into effect when the times will have reached their fulfillment—to bring all things in heaven and on earth together under one head, even Christ" (Ephesians 1:4-10).

What God is "guilty" of is none other than pre-planned, premeditated salvation. He's guilty of *loving* you, though He is generally accused of anything *but* that.

From the words that I have placed in the upper case in the above passage, we can learn something about God and His salvation.

CHOSE: You have been *chosen*.

BEFORE: Way ahead of time—before you were born or ever sinned.

ADOPTED: Salvation is a family matter.

PLEASURE: God enjoys His work.

GRACE: You don't deserve to be saved, but He wants to do it anyway.

LAVISHED: Undeserved favor—not sprinkled, but *poured out*.

WISDOM: Saving you makes good sense to God.

UNDERSTANDING: He knows what He's getting Himself into.

MYSTERY: The angels are learning along with us.

IN CHRIST: The only way anyone will ever be saved.

God has a plan, and it encompasses the entire human race. "He is patient with you, not wanting anyone to perish, but *everyone* to come to repentance" (2 Peter 3:9). God "wants *all* men to be saved and to come to a knowledge of the truth" (1 Timothy 2:4). "The grace of God that brings salvation has appeared to *all* men" (Titus 2:11). Christ died, not just for a few select individuals, but "for the sins of the *whole world*" (1 John 2:2). Let's face it: God is not partial in choosing whom He wants to save. He wants to save us ALL.

The truth is, hell is reserved for the devil and his demons *only*. God never meant for a single one of us to be there. It is a real tragedy that many of us would choose death over life, and end up there. Instead, God wishes heaven to be filled with all of humanity.

In insurance language, God has *comprehensive* coverage. And you can't beat the retirement benefits! Eternity is a *long* time—and no taxes, sickness, death, violence, poverty, pain, or loneliness live there.

In case you haven't noticed, this world is quite antagonistic towards us. Physically, our bodies begin to age while they are still relatively young. We can't be sure of even the air we breathe. And when we conquer one disease, another more devastating one takes its place.

Socially, we are a mess. Hatred and prejudice still abound, even though we can do marvelous things with computers and satellites. Our families are being torn apart. Economically, we are unstable and a person can lose his lifetime investment in a single moment. Mentally, we are a nervous wreck. Stress kills in numerous ways. Everything, it seems, is going against us in this life.

But not so spiritually. *Spiritually* everything is going *for* us. That's right. God has surrounded this race with an atmosphere of grace. Day and night He is busy influencing us along spiritual lines—presenting object lessons to us through life's circumstances. All of heaven has been employed for our salvation.

Every kindness that we show to others—every helpful word or deed—is prompted by His Spirit. Every sorrow for sin or desire to do right is evidence that His Spirit is moving upon our hearts. God never tires! He is at once aggressive and tender. And He is intimately involved with us—not afar off. He has gone out of His way to reach us. If we do not resist, *we shall be drawn to Him.**

What Surprises the Angels

What initially surprised the angels was that God actually followed through with His plan. They watched, in a state of holy shock, as the King of the universe put off His royal garments and proceeded to clothe Himself with humanity.

They watched Jesus throughout His short lifetime, and, especially during His public ministry, gained vivid insights into God's tremendous love for humankind. They must have felt helpless viewing the Savior in agony upon the cross, knowing they could not interfere. The scene was difficult enough to look upon, but hearing all

---

*For the basic thought of this paragraph and the previous, I am indebted to one of my favorite Christian authors, E.G. White, in the book *Steps to Christ* (Mountain View, CA: Pacific Press Pub. Assn. 1948), pp. 24, 30, 31. To receive a free copy of this fantastic little book, see order form in back of this book.

those jeers and expressions of hatred toward Him must have been unbearable. It will surely take them and us an eternity of education to begin to grasp just "how wide and long and high and deep is the love of Christ" (Ephesians 3:18). Indeed, "Even angels long to look into these things" (1 Peter 1:12).

What surprises them even more is the fact that, unfortunately, most of us will not accept His salvation, so freely given. This, too, they will try to figure out throughout eternity. But I am sure the aforementioned topic will be a far more popular and uplifting theme to ponder.

God the Initiator

Salvation involves a relationship, and God has already initiated it. He has made the first move. All we can ever do is *respond* in favor of or against His love.

God has "predestined" you to be saved—to be part of His eternal kingdom. He wishes above all things that you would accept His plan for you. But, unlike the enemy Satan, it is against God's nature to *force* your will. Your response, then, becomes vitally important.

You can't out-*feel* God, because He empathizes with the entire world. You can't out-*hurt* Him, because He is undergoing massive, large-scale rejection. You can't out-*smart* Him either, because He'll have a consuming response to every single line of defensive intellect you can muster. He is THERE, He is POISED, He is DETERMINED TO WIN YOUR HEART, and He simply must be dealt with.

Chapter 3

WHY RUNNING DOESN'T WORK

My Story

I was raised by a godly mother, who always provided a reassuring smile and a hopeful outlook. Like so many families of today, our's was a "broken" one. Most of the time it was just Mom and me.

We weren't really church-goers, but our little household was built upon Judeo-Christian values. I was a good kid, with an active conscience. When word came that an evangelistic crusade was starting in our area, we inquisitively attended.

I ate up those meetings. They were exciting. I learned so much in so little time. Life took on new meaning for my mother and me. We were both baptized, and in the days that followed we would go door to door telling our neighbors that Jesus loved them and that He was coming back real soon. I was 12.

My teen years were rough, as they are for many. I almost made it through them unscathed by drugs and alcohol. But the difficulties of the time, loneliness, the need of acceptance and the desire of escape, all combined to effectively push me over the edge. I discovered that I could create my own little world with minimal effort. Various drugs provided an effective, though temporary crutch for several years beyond high school. I had left the Christ of my childhood behind, and He had left me too, or so I thought.

Music was also a crutch for me. Perhaps it was the biggest. I had been writing songs for some time, mostly to express my longing for love and meaning. It wasn't a hobby. It was more a matter of survival. Through music I learned about myself and I saw a me that scared me to death. It was a self-centered, hedonistic, desperate person who wrote those songs. I did the most natural thing a person in my situation could do: I joined a band.

There were three bands, actually, but there was something quite different about the members of these bands: They were Christians.

I discovered that Christians had their share of problems too. The difference was, I was *smothered* by mine, while they took their's to Christ. I was drowning in my problems, but they seemed able to rise above life's situations as though some unseen hand was lifting them.

I found myself singing about God to others who needed to know Him, and yet I myself did not really know Him. I was a true hypocrite. But the Lord reached down and touched me through the songs I was then writing. He was capturing me within my own medium of expression. He was violating my own personal sphere. My soul began to ache.

He even allowed some drug dealers to break into my alley apartment and steal just about everything that was worth anything. I remember coming home from work to discover bare spaces where once treasured possessions had been. I felt angry, resentful, and then . . . empty. My identity had been wrapped up in those "things." Now part of me was gone.

I remember taking my dusty Bible off the shelf, slouching down in an old easy chair that was too ugly to be stolen, and opening to the book of Matthew. After scanning a few pages, my eyes fell upon these words: "Do not store up for yourselves treasures on earth, where moth and rust destroy, and where thieves break in and steal. But store up for yourselves treasures in heaven, where moth and rust do not destroy, and where thieves do not break in and steal. For where your treasure is, there your heart will be also" (6:19-21).

I was gripped with the fact that my heart had followed after the pleasures of sin, and that for all my searching I was really nowhere. My heart belonged in heaven, and Jesus Christ wanted to become my treasured Possession. And that He did.

My life was restored that day. A joy filled my heart that I have not been able to express. I learned to lean on—to put all my weight on Christ, for He is strong, and His strength is made perfect in my weakness (2 Corinthians 12:9).

I was forgiven, washed clean, enabled to stand and then to walk—a free man. He had always been after me—persistently pursuing me, loving me. I simply let Him in. The drugs departed, and the music was full of experiential joy! I couldn't contain myself. I had to tell others about my newly found Friend, who would not let me go.

Kinds of "Running"

It has been said that there is a God-shaped hole inside each of us. There is an inborn yearning for the truth—a hunger and a thirst that cannot be satisfied by any meal. Yet we try to fill up this hole—we try to satisfy this hunger and quench this thirst in numerous ways.

For me it was the use of drugs and a deep probing into *self*. Others try to fill that vacancy with an erotic lifestyle full of insatiable lust. For still others it is wealth, the "job" (workaholism), sports, eating, working out, dressing fit to kill, or even religion.

The list can go on and on. These are all forms of *running*. We are all runners in the sense that we tend to run away from God, though our lives ache for Him. We'll invest ourselves in just about anything, just so we can fill up that space inside without having to deal with the great I AM. But we really aren't satisfied. The thirst remains, and we grow restless.

The Lord sums it up quite nicely in Jeremiah 2:13: "'My people have committed two sins: They have forsaken me, the spring of living water, and have dug their own cisterns, *broken* cisterns that cannot hold water.'"

He is aware of our situation. Not only do we neglect Him, but we seek to *replace* Him with that which we *think* is a better source of life. Surely our running shoes are shot.

But I am so glad that my heavenly Father doesn't merely describe our situation. He goes beyond a mere appraisal. He actually offers a solution, in the form of an invitation: "The Spirit and the bride say, 'Come!' Whoever is thirsty, let him come; and whoever wishes, let him take the free gift of the water of life" (Revelation 22:17).

"Jesus answered, 'Everyone who drinks this water [our various addictions] will be thirsty again, but whoever drinks the water I give him will *never thirst*. Indeed, the water I give him will become in him a spring of water welling up to eternal life'" (John 4:13, 14).

Why do we insist on settling for a mere existence when we could be *truly living?* Jesus said, "I have come that they may have *life,* and have it to the *full*" (John 10:10).

In the abundant life that Christ offers, there is abundant peace, abundant meaning, abundant direction, and abundant security. You can run all you want, but I can attest to the fact that ONLY JESUS SATISFIES.

Two Examples of "Runners"

Our first runner is a "rich young man." Though we are not given his name, we are allowed to witness his encounter with Jesus Christ, as told in Mark 10:17-22. "As Jesus started on his way, a man ran up to him and fell on his knees before him. 'Good Teacher,' he asked, 'what must I do to inherit eternal life?'" Apparently in his running he had heard of this miracle-worker whom some believed to be the anticipated Messiah. As is often the case, His running somehow brought him face to face with Jesus.

This man, though young, held a position of responsibility. And he was rich. Yet he was not satisfied. Evidently he had seen something in Jesus that he himself did not have. He had witnessed the kindness that Jesus exhibited toward others. He had heard the words of authority spoken in love. And he had heard of the mighty miracles this Jesus had performed—not for Himself—but on behalf of those in need. Hence, he had come to view this Jesus as a respectable teacher, and a desire was growing in his heart: he wanted to become Jesus' disciple.

In reply to his question, Jesus told him that if he wanted to enter into life he must keep the commandments of God, and He quoted several of them which reveal man's duty to his neighbor.

"'Teacher,' he declared, 'all these I have kept since I was a boy.'" But instead of arguing with the young man, the Bible says that "Jesus looked at him and *loved* him." And then He offered the man eternal life in place of his particular mode of running. You could call it a test. "One thing you lack,' he said, 'Go, sell everything you have and give to the poor, and you will have treasure in heaven. Then come, follow me.'"

It was a test of discipleship. It happens to each of us. Whatever thing it is that we are clinging to for life instead of God—*that* is where the test will meet us.

"At this the man's face fell. He went away sad, because he had great wealth." His life could have been radically changed that very day. But the choice had presented itself, and the young man had declined Christ's invitation. He chose to keep running.

Our second runner is a man named "Saul." Saul had everything going for him. Here is how he describes himself: "Circumcised on the eighth day, of the people of Israel, of the tribe of Benjamin, a Hebrew of Hebrews; in regard to the law, a Pharisee; as for zeal, persecuting the church; as for legalistic righteousness, faultless" (Philippians 3:5, 6).

Saul was an intellectual, trained at the feet of one of the foremost teachers of his day—Gemaliel. Saul was a scholar. But he was also a Pharisee, and Pharisees prided themselves in their external obedience. Not only did they endeavor to obey every law which God had put forth through Moses;

they also *added on* their own particulars as baggage. But inwardly, they did not experience a renewed heart. They took advantage of widows and the poor. They sought to make a profit off the "temple tax."

Saul was also a ruthless murderer of Christians. He would go out of his way to find followers of Jesus—taking them as prisoners to Jerusalem for trial, where he would personally bear witness to their death.

But one day as Saul was on one of his "Christian hunts"—headed for Damascus—"suddenly a light from heaven flashed around him. He fell to the ground and heard a voice say to him, 'Saul, Saul, why do you persecute me?'

'Who are you, Lord?' Saul asked.

'I am Jesus, whom you are persecuting,' he replied. 'Now get up and go into the city, and you will be told what you must do'" (Acts 9:3-6).

Saul's running had been in the form of self-righteousness, position, pride, and accomplishment. Then he suddenly met the Lord of the people he was murdering. He was blinded by the light of the risen Christ.

How did he respond to Jesus' words? Unlike our first runner, Saul decided to follow Jesus—to stop running. Here is how he describes it: "But whatever was to my profit I now consider loss for the sake of Christ. What is more, I consider everything a loss compared to the surpassing greatness of knowing Christ Jesus my Lord, for whose sake I have lost all things" (Philippians 3:7, 8).

Saul became Paul; a mighty apostle and warrior for God during the infancy of His church. Paul never looked back. Being a disciple of Jesus meant everything to him. What an impact he had on his world! Even today—after 1900 years—

his letters change lives and compel people to think deeply about spiritual matters. And all because of a single choice that he made. The choice to stop running and start following.

The Futility of Boasting

Sir Isaac Newton was WISE. He was one of the world's most renowned philosophers, mathematicians, and scholars. He even delved into the prophecies of the Bible. It has been said that he surpassed the whole human race in genius. And yet when requested in his declining days to explain some passage in his chief mathematical work, he could only reply that "he knew it was true *once.*" He had forgotten what his own writing meant. **"Let not the wise man boast of his wisdom"** (Jeremiah 9:23a).

Napoleon Bonaparte was STRONG. He pronounced himself emperor of France in 1804, and pictured himself on a par with Alexander the Great and Caesar; a conqueror and a ruler. Had Napoleon wished it, Europe might have had peace. But his ambition would not permit it.

In a single decade, Napoleon conquered most of Europe in a series of military campaigns that astonished the world. He would put as many as 700,000 men under arms at one time, risk as many as 100,000 troops in a single battle, endure heavy losses, and come back to fight again.

His aim was not to control territory nor to gain strong points, but to destroy the enemy army. No single enemy could match Napoleon's military strength. But on June 18, 1815, in the Battle of Waterloo, Napoleon Bonaparte was defeated by the Duke of Wellington's combined forces. **". . . or the strong man boast of his strength"** (Jeremiah 9:23b).

J.P. Morgan, Sr. was RICH. Fabulously rich. He was an extremely successful financier. But when he was on his deathbed, the marks of anxiety were upon his countenance. He who had *millions* had not *peace*.

When asked by those in attendance if there was anything that could be done to make him more comfortable, he replied, "No, but I desire that prayer be offered in my behalf before I die."

He had among his acquaintances many of the world's most illustrious leaders, but as these were named, one by one, he slowly shook his head. "Where is the gardener?" he asked. "He is a man who prays, and God hears him. Call the gardener."

And so the humble gardener with gnarled hands and sunburned face was summoned. He passed through the rich man's opulent mansion, to the place where J.P. Morgan lay. Then the gardener prayed, and as he prayed, Morgan grew composed, for he believed in that man, and he knew that God heard him. And when the prayer was finished, he uttered the simple sentence, "It is well."

". . . or the rich man boast of his riches, but let him who boasts boast about this: that he understands and knows me, that I am the Lord, who exercises kindness, justice and righteousness on earth, for in these I delight" (Jeremiah 9:23c, 24).

- -

Salvation is a relational matter. What is most important, in the final analysis, is not what you know, or how much you know. It's *who* you know.

Chapter 4

THE CHRIST WHO CRIES WITH YOU

Anyone who has lived at all in this world has suffered in some way. Suffering is alien to no culture or time. It is fond of all ages and classes, and manifests itself in the countenances of people near and far. It is simply part of the human situation.

This chapter does not seek to answer all of the questions one could ask about suffering. It does offer a few principles that might prove helpful; things that should be considered when thinking about suffering and those who suffer.

Where It Came From

"And there was war in heaven. Michael and his angels fought against the dragon, and the dragon and his angels fought back. But he was not strong enough, and they lost their place in heaven. The great dragon was hurled down—that ancient serpent called the devil or Satan, who leads the whole world astray. He was hurled to the earth, and his angels with him" (Revelation 12:7-9).

The first war. And it wasn't even on this planet. And God didn't start it. This is the point. GOD IS NOT THE AUTHOR OF SUFFERING. The dragon here represents Satan, also known as Lucifer and the "serpent," which is a fitting term. We are given a glimpse of what caused war to break out in heaven:

"How you have fallen from heaven, O morning star, son of the dawn! You have been cast down to the earth. . . . You said in your heart, 'I will ascend to heaven; I will raise my throne above the stars of God; I will sit enthroned on the mount of assembly, on the utmost heights of the sacred mountain. I will ascend above the tops of the clouds; I will make myself like the Most High.' But you are brought down to the grave, to the depths of the pit" (Isaiah 14:12-15).

Lucifer wanted to play God, but only God can be God. Even though he was the highest, most honored angel in heaven, Lucifer was still an *angel*. And angels are created beings.

The discord that Lucifer spread among the angelic host was devastating: one-third of them actually believed his lies about God and about His Son. And so where once peace reigned supreme there was war, started by a pride trip.

The fact that suffering exists at all is evidence of a power at work other than God. When the Lord created this world it was *good*. There was no *suffering* until the onset of *sin*. The two go together like flies and garbage heaps. There is no suffering outside the atmosphere of sin, and there is no sin without a Satan.

So this whole mess was started not by God, but by Satan. I think we should give him credit for that which he causes.

God the Sufferer

In fact, the Bible paints quite a *different* picture of God. It is a picture of a Sufferer. "O Jerusalem, Jerusalem, you who kill the prophets and stone those sent to you, how often I have longed to gather your children together, as a hen gathers her chicks under her wings, but you were not willing" (Matthew 23:37).

Can you picture Christ crying over His own people, although He was just about to be murdered by them? Don't you think that most of us would have our own misfortune on our minds?

The Creator of everything good gave up His life, suffering all the way. He suffered not only physical pain, but emotional pain, the pain of rejection, and the pain of being separated from His Father because our sins were upon Him. Then there is the special kind of pain that only God can experience when taking upon Himself a human body. Though He was truly man, His *God*ness recoiled from the sinful perversions and cruelties He witnessed during His life. Such pain we cannot begin to imagine.

Why didn't God just wipe Satan out of existence a long time ago, before the earth was created? Because it wouldn't have solved anything. There would always be suspicion in the air. The angels would have wondered if perhaps Satan's accusations were right after all—that God is nothing but a tyrant and that His laws are unfair.

No, the only way to forever silence the voice of sinful rebellion was to let it run its course. Let everybody see just how ugly sin really is. Let everybody see the true character of God. Lay them side by side in human history—hate and love, discord and unity, destruction and growth, confusion and peace. Let the universe understand these issues, and sin won't happen a second time.

God could have *forced* all those rebellious angels to love and obey Him. He could have made robots out of them. He could have, but He refused to. Because He would have violated one of His most important principles: Freedom of Choice.

It is not like God to force the will. He who has all power would never think of forcing you or me to follow Him. He does not want obligated or pre-programmed disciples. He does not rule by coercion. He simply knocks on the door of our hearts (Revelation 3:20).

The devil, on the other hand, makes a habit of breaking down the door, sneaking in through the window, or picking the lock. He does not care about freedom of choice. He will do whatever it takes to control your life, and he will get you to believe that he really isn't when he actually is.

How important is your freedom of choice to God? It means everything to Him. He does not want rebellion to occur a second time. The people that will inhabit heaven and the new earth will be there because they *want* to be, not because they are forced to be.

To what extent will God go to protect your freedom of choice? He would rather DIE than force you to love Him. And that He did.

"Jesus Wept"

Lazarus, Mary, and Martha were siblings. They were very good friends of Jesus, who would often go to their home to rest and recuperate from His busy schedule. But one day Jesus was sent word that Lazarus was very ill.

Instead of leaving immediately for Bethany, Jesus lingered where He was for two more days. He told His disciples that something good was going to come out of this particular suffering. The eleventh chapter of John contains the story, and as it goes, Lazarus actually dies, and Jesus knows it.

When He finally arrives, Lazarus has already been in the tomb for several days. Martha goes out to meet Jesus, and asks Him why He did not come sooner, so that Lazarus would not have had to die. To this Jesus replies, "Your brother will rise again" (Verse 23).

Then Mary also comes out and asks Him the same question. And when Jesus sees her weeping and all of the friends and family weeping, *He weeps also*.

This is something we need to remember. GOD SUFFERS WITH US. He is not ashamed of us nor our situation. He does not wish to distance Himself from us when we suffer. Instead, He chooses to cry with us, and wants more than anything for us to lean on His shoulder, and let Him carry our burden.

Jesus was indeed touched that day by all the sadness. But He was also weeping over their lack of faith. Because that very hour He would raise a dead Lazarus from the tomb! The "Resurrection and the Life" was in their midst— He who held the keys to death. When Jesus shouted, "Lazarus, come forth," it was a perfectly restored Lazarus who walked out of the tomb—grave cloths and all.

Sometimes God allows there to be suffering in our lives, but it is because there is a *greater miracle* that He wants to bring out of the situation. God deals in multiple blessings. That is, He wants to affect more than one person at the same time.

The Bible has a lot to say about suffering. Here is one example: "Consider it pure joy, my brothers, whenever you face trials of many kinds, because you know that the testing of your faith develops perseverance. Perseverance must finish its work so that you may be mature and complete, not lacking anything" (James 1:2-4).

Although He is not the Author of suffering, God will orchestrate things in such a way that we can be drawn closer to Him *through* the suffering. Our maturity and growth depend on how we handle the trials that meet us. If we believe that God is an orchestrator, we will believe His Word when it says, "In all things God works for the good of those who love him" (Romans 8:28).

God the Healer

Jesus was passing through Samaria. He was tired and thirsty after walking for several hours in the hot sun. He came upon Jacob's well, and sat down to rest.

The fourth chapter of John contains the story. A Samaritan woman came to the well to draw water, but little did she know that Jesus had been thinking about her throughout His journey that morning. Jesus started the conversation.

"'Will you give me a drink?' (His disciples had gone into the town to buy food.)"

"The Samaritan woman said to him, 'You are a Jew and I am a Samaritan woman. How can you ask me for a drink?' (For Jews do not associate with Samaritans.)"

"Jesus answered her, 'If you knew the gift of God and who it is that asks you for a drink, you would have asked him and he would have given you living water.'"

"'Sir,' the woman said, 'you have nothing to draw with and the well is deep. Where can you get this living water? Are you greater than our father Jacob, who gave us the well and drank from it himself, as did also his sons and his flocks and herds?'"

"Jesus answered, 'Everyone who drinks this water will be thirsty again, but whoever drinks the water I give him will never thirst. Indeed, the water I give him will become in him a spring of water welling up to eternal life.'"

The woman was preoccupied with nationalism, but Jesus looked beyond race and culture. The woman was focused on the temporal, but Jesus sought to lift her into the eternal. What He had to offer her was much more lasting and refreshing than mere water. He offered Himself.

But here is where we see how completely Christ wants to save us. This woman would not be able to make progress spiritually until she faced her past. There were wounds there that needed healing, and Jesus knew it.

"'Go, call your husband and come back.'"

"'I have no husband,' she replied."

"Jesus said to her, "You are right when you say you have no husband. The fact is, you have had five husbands, and the man you now have is not your husband.'"

"'Sir,' the woman said, 'I can see you are a prophet.'"

Was Jesus trying to put the woman on the spot? Was He trying to rub her face in her past? No. But you have to admit it certainly got her attention. Now she was relating to him on a different level. Now He was more to her than a tired philosophical Jew. He *knew* her.

The story indeed has a great ending. The "woman at the well" went and told the people of her town about this man who helped her face her past, her pain. Many of those Samaritans believed in Jesus because of her testimony.

But what is the point? What does this incident tell us about Christ, and at the same time about God? For "God was reconciling the world to himself in Christ" (2 Corinthians 5:19).

The point is that God is willing to take us by the hand and walk us through those hurts of yesteryear, if they are impacting negatively upon our present life. God is in the business of healing; of restoring broken hearts and broken homes. His awesome power can break the patterns of despair, so the past doesn't have to be repeated. His healing love can mend our shattered dreams, so we can dare to be all that we were meant to be.

Hope. It is a fundamental human need. You cannot truly live without it. And God through Christ is giving it to you. He who spoke the word, and the heavens came into existence, also spoke another Word, and that "Word became flesh and lived for a while among us. We have seen his glory, the glory of the one and only Son, who came from the Father, full of grace and truth" (John 1:14).

Wherever life finds you just now, you can be assured that Christ is with you, taking in your situation in its entirety, seeing the end from the beginning, knowing you fully, and loving you just the same. Do not be afraid of His presence. Be thankful that the greatest power in the universe is not hatred, but the kind of love that would willingly, unselfishly hang upon a cross for you. This is the kind of Christ who sits beside you now, matching tear for tear.

Chapter 5

HOW TO BE BORN

An Accomplished Act in History

When God speaks, things happen. Salvation occurs. We now have the privilege of looking back through time to a specific Friday afternoon, when Jesus the Son of God willingly gave up His life on a cross. Crucifixion was the usual means of executing common criminals. Jesus was treated as one of those, for us.

"He himself bore our sins in his body on the tree, so that we might die to sins and live to righteousness; by his wounds you have been healed" (1 Peter 2:24). It actually happened. Ancient Jewish and secular writers like Josephus, Pliny the Younger, Cornelius Tacitus, and Hadrian all make mention of this Jew named Jesus.*

He was a real person who lived a real life, and died a real death for you.

---

*For an excellent book on the subject, see Josh McDowell and Bill Wilson, *He Walked Among Us: Evidence for the Historical Jesus,* (San Bernardino, CA: Here's Life, 1988). Available at your local Christian bookstore.

"God made him [Christ] who had no sin to be sin for us, so that in him we might become the righteousness of God" (2 Corinthians 5:21). This is the great swap of history. Jesus takes all our sins, and we take His righteousness. It doesn't make sense down here, because this world is so self-oriented. But it makes perfect sense in heaven.

Christ is our Substitute. Though He was perfect in all His ways, He allowed Himself to die in our place. He allowed Himself to be treated as the worst of sinners. We are all sinners through and through. We really deserve nothing more than the wages of sin. "For the wages of sin is death, but the gift of God is eternal life in Christ Jesus our Lord" (Romans 6:23).

Jesus died for us. When did He do it? At just the right time. "You see, at just the right time, when we were still powerless, Christ died for the ungodly. Very rarely will anyone die for a righteous man, though for a good man someone migh possibly dare to die. But God demonstrates his own love for us in this: While we were still sinners, Christ died for us" (Romans 5:6-8).

When did Jesus die for us? WHEN WE WERE STILL POWERLESS! WHEN WE WERE STILL RUNNING FROM HIM! At the weakest point in our lives, Christ died for us, in order to lift us up.

Being born again involves accepting the greatest act in history on your behalf.

By Grace Through Faith

"For it is by grace you have been saved, through faith—and this not from yourselves, it is the gift of God—not by works, so that no one can boast" (Ephesians 2:8, 9). At the cross, the entire human race is humbled. The cross is the great equalizer. We can bring nothing there to commend ourselves to God. Don't even try to earn your way to heaven; you can't. Each of us is in desperate need of salvation.

GRACE is undeserved favor or love. It is an acquittal, not of the innocent, but of the guilty; which is why it is called *amazing* grace. Grace means that God is willing to take your sins and *remove* them. Grace means that God is willing to relate to you as though you had no sin.

"He does not treat us as our sins deserve or repay us according to our iniquities. For as high as the heavens are above the earth, so great is his love for those who fear him; as far as the east is from the west, so far has he removed our transgressions from us" (Psalm 103:10-12).

The heavens stretch out for innumerable light years from earth. When gazing into the evening sky, we can see stars that are hundreds of millions of miles away. God wants to take all our sins and place them aboard a space shuttle, and program that shuttle to keep traveling through space, right past those stars, and never stop. Salvation is uni-directional. The Lord wants us to go one way, and our sins to go another. And He has the power to make that happen.

Grace is provided in the death of Jesus Christ. But how do you appropriate it? How do you *receive* grace? According to Ephesians chapter 2, FAITH is the hand that takes hold of grace.

Faith involves belief; we need to believe in the God who saves us. But believing that there is a God is not enough. The Bible says, "Even the demons believe that—and shudder" (James 2:19).

No, we must *trust* God as well. This is something that the demons would *never* do. This matter of trust can best be illustrated by the chair. Let's say someone gives you a chair. You look at it, and it appears to be strong. You touch its frame, and it is stable. All the screws seem to be in place. All four legs are intact and are not wobbly. "Yes," you say, "I *believe* this chair can hold me up." But is the chair *doing* anything for you yet? Absolutely not!

In order for that chair to be of any use to you, you must actually *sit down* on it—not just half way, supporting yourself partly by your feet still—but *all the way*. You must put all of your weight on the chair in order for it to do the job it was meant to do.

And so trusting Christ means putting ALL OF YOUR WEIGHT on Him—LEANING on Him. FAITH involves a trust relationship between you and Christ. That is how grace is received, and that is how grace is retained. Is it a cop-out? Not at all. We are trusting God to forgive us for Christ's sake. We are taking Him at His word, allowing Him to save us.

What if you don't have any faith? Christ thought about that too. Just ask Him, and He will give you faith, for He is "the author and perfecter of our faith" (Hebrews 12:2).

Repentance and Confession

"From that time on Jesus began to preach, 'Repent, for the kingdom of heaven is near.'" "'Repent, then, and turn to God, so that your sins may be wiped out, that times of refreshing may come from the Lord'" (Matthew 4:17; Acts 3:19).

Repentance is a deep sorrow for sin, and a turning away from it. But we cannot sorrow over our sin unless we see how ugly it is; unless we see what it did to the Son of God, and what it does to our lives. This is the job of the Holy Spirit, who is the presence of God in your life.

The Spirit Himself shows us the hideous nature of sin. The Spirit creates in us a longing to be cleansed of our sins, and a determination to turn from our sins.

Repentance, like faith, is a gift of God. "God exalted him [Christ] to his own right hand as Prince and Savior that he might give repentance and forgiveness of sins to Israel" (Acts 5:31). So if you don't think you have repentance, ask Jesus for some, and He will give it to you. After all, it's His kindness that *leads* us to repentance (Romans 2:4).

Confession is the act of acknowledging your sins to those you have sinned against. In other words, we confess our sins to people, and to God. Why not just to God? Because God is interested in our relationships. He wants to bring healing to every part of our life—the horizontal plane (the people in our life), and the vertical plane (our relationship with God).

There is a very powerful promise that has to do with confession. "If we confess our sins, he is faithful and just and will forgive us our sins and purify us from all unrighteousness" (1 John 1:9). You can't get any plainer than that. God is serious about restoring our lives, if we will simply talk with Him about our lives.

Assurance

Everybody needs assurance. In fact, most of us need *re*assurance. That's why the Lord put 1 John chapter 5 in the Bible. "And this is the testimony: God has GIVEN us eternal life, and this life is in his Son. HE WHO HAS THE SON HAS LIFE; he who does not have the Son of God does not have life. I write these to you who believe in the name of the

Son of God so that you may KNOW that you have eternal life" (1 John 5:11-13).

There are three key ideas in this passage. First of all, we simply must get it through our heads that eternal life is a GIFT. There is absolutely no way we can ever earn it or buy it. We are sinners, and the only wages that sin earns is death. We will not progress to a point at which we can say we've arrived, and so rightly deserve to inherit eternity.

To receive eternal life, we simply must *take* it. It is waiting there in the nail-scarred palm of Jesus Christ. He's holding it out to you. Just take it.

Secondly, if you have the Son, my friend you have *life*. Jesus said, "'I am the way and the truth and the life. No one comes to the Father except through me'" (John 14:6). To "have" Jesus means to accept Him as Savior and Lord. These terms will be discussed in the very next section.

Thirdly, if we are in Christ we can indeed KNOW that we have eternal life. There should be no doubt in our hearts. Our personal acceptance of the death and resurrection of Jesus Christ on our behalf makes eternal life a *certainty!* We should not wait to *feel* like we are saved, but should base our lives on the plain Word of God.

Christ as Savior and Lord

To accept Christ as our personal SAVIOR, we must believe that He died FOR US, IN OUR PLACE. Christ took our sins upon Himself, and actually died our death. If we refuse to accept Jesus as Savior, then we will one day die a death that lasts forever. But accepting Christ's death in our place means that we will only die a physical, temporary death; not a spiritual, eternal death.

In fact, there is a very real possibility that we will not die *at all*, because, according to Bible prophecy, we are very close to the Second Coming of Jesus Christ. On that day He will come to take His people home. It will be the most glorious day of your life, *if* Jesus is the Friend you have been walking with up to that time.

To accept Christ as LORD, we must be willing to be His DISCIPLE. A disciple is one who follows another. We accept Jesus as our new Leader, and give up the control of our life to Him. We were never meant to govern our own affairs just as we see fit. The fact that so many people try to run their own lives is why there is so much chaos in the world.

The disciple allows his Master to have His way in every part of his life. This might seem to be a difficult thing to do, since we have so many secrets we don't want to share, and we cannot bear to give up certain treasured sins. But God already knows about these areas, and He wants to replace the bad with the good, the unhealthy with the healthy, the hurtful with that which heals, and the temporal with the eternal.

Following Jesus means we listen closely to what He has to say, just as His disciples of old did. Today we have the Bible as our guide for life. His opinion is contained there, and that opinion should *count* more than any other opinion in this world.

For instance, let's say you are thinking that you are not worth anything and that your life is going nowhere. Then you read in God's Word about how valuable you are, since the King of Kings died for you, and about a plan that God has for your life. Who are you to argue with God? You would have to relinquish your negative opinion of yourself and life, because you are a disciple of Christ.

How We Are Born

Nicodemus was a Pharisee who was a member of the Jewish ruling council. He wanted to meet with Jesus, but was afraid to be seen with Him during the day. So he came to Jesus by night. Here is part of their conversation:

"'Rabbi, we know you are a teacher who has come from God. For no one could perform the miraculous signs you are doing if God were not with Him.'

"In reply Jesus declared, 'I tell you the truth, unless a man is born again, he cannot see the kingdom of God.'"

"'How can a man be born when he is old?' Nicodemus asked. 'Surely he cannot enter a second time into his mother's womb to be born!'"

"Jesus answered, 'I tell you the truth, unless a man is born of water and the Spirit, he cannot enter the kingdom of God. Flesh gives birth to flesh, but the Spirit gives birth to spirit. You should not be surprised at my saying, You must be born again. The wind blows wherever it pleases. You hear its sound, but you cannot tell where it comes from or where it is going. So it is with everyone born of the Spirit'" (John 3:2-8).

We cannot exactly explain just how a person is born again, but we know that it is the Spirit's doing. There is a supernatural transformation in the person's life. "Therefore, if anyone is in Christ, he is a new creation; the old has gone, the new has come!" (2 Corinthians 5:17).

We must not wait to *feel* new. We must take God at His word and believe that we *are* new. Remember—we cannot *see* the new birth taking place, but we *can* see the changes in attitude and behavior that are *results* of the new birth. True life begins at the cross.

It is appropriate to speak of the birth *process*. Any mother who has labored with a child can tell you that birth does not happen all at once. And so if you, my friend, are struggling and going through some difficult times just now, consider it normal. Remember that babies come out of one world and enter another when they are born. It can be painful, and there will probably be tears, regardless of the gender.

We are BEING born. It is a daily experience; an ongoing process of growth with Christ our Savior.

A Prayer for Those Being Born

If you accept Jesus Christ as your Savior, and believe He died in your place; and if you accept Him as the Lord of your life, and wish to follow Him, pray this little prayer to God just now, where you are:

Dear Father
I realize I am a sinner
Thank you for sending Jesus to die in my place
Thank you Jesus for forgiving ALL my sins
Thank you for washing me and making me clean
Thank you for the gift of eternal life
I accept you as my Savior
I renounce my allegiance to the enemy Satan
And I acknowledge you as my Lord
Help me to follow you everyday
Help me to be a good disciple
Help me to obey what your Word says
Please send your Holy Spirit to guide me and comfort me

Help me to tell others of your love
And thank you for making me a new creation
In Jesus name, Amen.

Royalty

If you have just given your life to Christ, I want to take this opportunity to WELCOME you to the family of God! It's a ROYAL family; and you are ROYALTY, because you belong to the KING of the Universe! Here are a few "royal" passages:

"Yet to all who received him, to those who believed in his name, he gave the right to become children of God—children born not of natural descent, nor of human decision or a husband's will, but born of God" (John 1:12, 13).

"But because of his great love for us, God, who is rich in mercy, made us alive with Christ even when we were dead in transgressions—it is by grace you have been saved. And God raised us up with Christ and seated us with him in the heavenly realms in Christ Jesus, in order that in the coming ages he might show the incomparable riches of his grace, expressed in his kindness to us in Christ Jesus" (Ephesians 2:4-7).

"You are all sons of God through faith in Christ Jesus, for all of you who were baptized into Christ have clothed yourselves with Christ. . . .If you belong to Christ, then you are Abraham's seed, and heirs according to the promise" (Galatians 3:26, 27, 29).

A Word on Baptism

"Don't you know that all of us who were baptized into Christ Jesus were baptized into his death? We were therefore buried with him through baptism into death in order that, just as Christ was raised from the dead through the glory of the Father, we too may live a new life" (Romans 6:3, 4).

The word "baptize" means to "immerse or dip." Baptism is a very important step in the Christian life. Even Jesus was baptized, even though He was sinless. He did this to serve as our Example, that we should follow in His footsteps.

Baptism is an external sign of an internal decision. You don't become a Christian when you come up out of the water; you are already one before you ever enter the water. It is a public way of declaring your commitment to Jesus Christ.

Baptism represents the fact that you have died to your sins, which have been placed upon Jesus on the cross. The coming up out of the water signifies your "resurrection" into a new life, just as Christ was resurrected. In other words, in the rite of baptism the Christian identifies him- or herself with the death and resurrection of Jesus Christ. It is a public way of saying, "I accept these acts of Christ on my behalf."

You can say, along with the apostle Paul, "I have been crucified with Christ and I no longer live, but Christ lives in me. The life I live in the body, I live by faith in the Son of God, who loved me and gave himself for me" (Galatians 2:20).

When we are born of the Spirit into a new life with Jesus, we really do not lose our identity. Rather, we begin the process of becoming all we were meant to be. We become the real you, and the real me, because a real God has saved us.

Chapter 6

HOW TO WALK

S o then, just as you received Christ Jesus as Lord, continue to live in him, rooted and built up in him, strengthened in the faith as you were taught, and overflowing with thankfulness" (Colossians 2:6, 7).

We are to *live* in Christ just as we *received* Him. How did we receive Him? By *faith*. So we are to *continue* to trust our Savior—letting our roots go down deep into Him. This is how we grow as Christians.

Abiding in Christ

Let's take the "roots" analogy a step further. Listen to how Jesus explains our relationship with Him:

"'I am the vine; you are the branches. If a man remains in me and I in him, he will bear much fruit; apart from me you can do nothing. If anyone does not remain in me, he is like a branch that is thrown away and withers; such branches are picked up, thrown into the fire and burned. If you remain in me and my words remain in you, ask whatever you wish, and it will be given you. This is to my Father's glory, that you bear much fruit, showing yourselves to be my disciples'" (John 15:5-8).

Evidently a disciple is someone who *bears fruit*. But the fruitage comes through our "remaining" or "abiding" in the Vine, Jesus Christ. In fact, according to this passage it is impossible for us to bear fruit unless we are abiding in Christ.

Since abiding is so important, Jesus made sure He gave us the two essential ingredients to an abiding relationship. Here they are, in equation form:

PRAYER + WORD = ABIDE

The importance of this equation cannot be overstated. Jesus said, "If you remain in me." That's called PRAYER. Prayer is the Christian's lifeblood. We have the privilege of pouring our hearts out to our God at any time of the day. We can talk with Him about big things and little things; complex things and simple things. He is extremely interested in us, and He loves to commune with His children through prayer.

Jesus also said, "and my words remain in you." That's reflection upon the Word of God—the Holy Bible. Written by about 40 different writers over hundreds of years, the Bible is amazingly cohesive in its thrust. There is a golden thread of truth weaving its way throughout this holy Book. Though many topics are touched upon, the central theme of the Bible is the plan of redemption—the restoration of the image of God in the human soul. This is accomplished through our complete dependence upon Jesus Christ, and our obedience to his Word.

Many people have given their lives in the effort to make the Bible available in the common languages of the world. Look how useful this Book is: "All Scripture is God-breathed and is useful for teaching, rebuking, correcting and training in righteousness, so that the man of God may be thoroughly equipped for every good work" (2 Timothy 3:16, 17).

Every morning we have the privilege of starting brand new with Christ. Daily devotions are to the disciple as gas is to the car. You simply will not get very far spiritually unless you are daily in prayer and the reading of the Word.

For starters, I highly recommend the Gospel of John, because of its personal nature. Read a little each day, and wherever you see Jesus talking to someone, replace that person's name with your own, mentally. This will help you to take to heart every word Christ speaks. You'll hear Him talking to *you*. You will be a participant, not a spectator.

Remember that quantity is not as important as quality. It really doesn't matter how much you read. The Bible is a *spiritual* book. Do not try to read it as you would a text book, or a novel. There are magnificent insights to be gained in every passage. A single verse can occupy your thoughts all through the day.

You will also want to *memorize* certain verses that are especially meaningful to you. You'll be surprised at the strength you will draw from these passages during the day. Write the verse down on a little index card and carry it with you, looking at it now and then, until you've got it committed to memory. Don't be shocked when the Lord places someone in your path with whom you can share that memorized verse. Remember He deals in multiple blessings.

Always pray for the Spirit's guidance before you read the Bible. He is the real Author, and He can open your mind to the timeless truths that are written there. Here again is that fundamental equation you should keep in mind:

PRAYER + WORD = ABIDE

The Promise of Fruit

Through prayer and the reading of His Word, we abide in Christ. Jesus said that we would bear much fruit if we abide in Him. What He was talking about is the "fruit of the Spirit." These are qualities of character that every Christian will automatically have, through an abiding relationship with Christ.

In Galatians chapter 5 we are given two lists: the acts of the sinful nature, and the fruit of the Spirit. These lists are not necessarily exhaustive, but serve as examples. Let's look at the first list, the acts of the sinful nature:

"The acts of the sinful nature are obvious: sexual immorality, impurity and debauchery; idolatry and witchcraft, hatred, discord, jealousy, fits of rage, selfish ambition, dissensions, factions and envy; drunkenness, orgies, and the like. I warn you, as I did before, that those who live like this will not inherit the kingdom of God" (Galatians 5:19-21).

Paul is not known for his mincing of words. He is very straightforward, for our own good. Before we come to Christ, these characteristics are part of our lives, in varying degrees. But notice the second list, the fruit of the Spirit, found in the next three verses:

"But the fruit of the Spirit is love, joy, peace, patience, kindness, goodness, faithfulness, gentleness and self-control. Against such things there is no law. Those who belong to Christ Jesus have crucified the sinful nature with its passions and desires" (Galatians 5:22-24).

It isn't hard to see that these fruit of the Spirit are the very opposite of the acts of the sinful nature. These are GOOD THINGS! Many people would give anything for these fruit. Most people do not have them, because we are not *born* with them; they are *acquired*. They are given to us by God's Spirit, as we abide in Jesus Christ, the Vine.

You can think of the Lord Jesus as a Surgeon. He surgically removes the acts of the sinful nature from our lives, one by one. But He does not leave gaping holes in our lives. Rather, as He removes one act of the sinful nature, He *replaces* it with one of the fruit of the Spirit. He does not replace everything all at once, because that would overwhelm us. He knows when we are ready to make progress in a new area. Remember: fruit *develops*.

Jesus made it clear that He is the Vine, and we are the branches. We are totally dependent on Him for everything in life. Our nourishment is drawn from Him. And if we maintain our contact with Him through prayer (our voice to Him) and the reading of His Word (His voice to us), He will add these wonderful fruit to our lives.

Fellowship and Witnessing

Along with prayer and the reading of the Word, two other important aspects of Christian growth are fellowship and witnessing. Regarding fellowship, the Bible has this to say: "Let us not give up meeting together, as some are in the habit of doing, but let us encourage one another—and all the more as you see the Day approaching" (Hebrews 10:25).

Believers need each other. We are not saved in a vacuum. God saves us in a community, called a church. Don't confuse the building with the church. The PEOPLE OF GOD are what comprise the church. You can have a church without any building whatsoever, although it is nice to be able to pray or sing a song without getting rained on.

We are supposed to uplift and strengthen each other. That is part of God's plan. Fellowship includes praying, sharing, laughing, crying, playing, and studying together. There is no substitute for it. Now and then you may want to be alone with God in nature. But if you do not return to the community of believers, you simply will not live life to the fullest; and you will be deliberately sinning against your God. Your presence is desperately needed in the church. You have something unique to offer, and we will touch more on this in chapter 8. Just remember that God saves us *together*.

Witnessing is also important. Jesus said, "'Whoever acknowledges me before men, I will also acknowledge him before my Father in heaven. But whoever disowns me before men, I will disown him before my Father in heaven" (Matthew 10:32). This is a serious matter. Jesus is not ashamed to present our case before the Father, saying, "This is my disciple. I shed my blood for this person." Can we be too ashamed to share Him with others?

Actually, witnessing comes natural to the heart that has been healed. We cannot help but tell others of the saving grace of Christ, the peace He gives, and the power He has to transform. Every time we share our testimony we strengthen our own faith, and our own experience.

Dealing with Temptation

Unfortunately, temptation is part of our earthly life. We will have to confront our sinful natures for the rest of our lives, even though we have been born again. The carnal nature is not destroyed when we accept Jesus, but it *is rendered powerless.* For every temptation that meets us, whether from within or from without, GOD HAS PROVIDED A WAY OF ESCAPE:

"No temptation has seized you except what is common to man. And God is faithful; he will not let you be tempted beyond what you can bear. But when you are tempted, he will also provide a way out so that you can stand up under it" (1 Corinthians 10:13).

There are two important points here: (1) You'll never meet any temptation that you and God cannot handle, and, (2) There is *always* a way of escape; just look for it. I will let you in on a little secret that has helped me. We are told in 1 Thessalonians 5:17 to "pray continually." This doesn't mean we should go around all day with our eyes closed and our heads bowed. It *does* mean that we should always be in an *attitude* of prayer. In other words, keeping Christ in the forefront of our thinking—knowing He is with us.

This is a kind of communion that I have with my Savior. It's called living in the presence of God, and it works. When I am tempted, Christ is right there, ready to do battle for me. Since we are engaged in an ongoing conversation of sorts, my request for help and the arrival of His aid package are simultaneous events. He shows me the way of escape, and if I am serious about growth, I follow.

Sometimes the way of escape is simply looking the other way. Sometimes it means refusing to follow through on a certain thought. You see, it is not a sin to be tempted. It *is* a sin to *entertain* a temptation; that is, to give it the time of day, or to dwell on it or act on it.

James 4:7 says, "Submit yourselves, then, to God. Resist the devil, and he will flee from you." To submit is to surrender. If there is anyone the devil hates it's a Christian who realizes his own weakness, and submits to God. The devil knows he is no match for Almighty God. He takes a hike, partly because he isn't stupid, and partly because when you submit to God a host of holy angels are sent to your rescue. *Please* remember this vital truth:

SUBMIT AND RESIST

The greatest battle the Christian faces is the battle of SELF. When our common parents Adam and Eve started distrusting God's Word and doubting that God's way was truly best for them, Christ was kicked off the throne of the heart, and *self* climbed on. Ever since that time, Christ has been trying to get Himself back on the throne of the heart, by waging war on *self*.

By "self" we mean the sinful nature. The reason why the world is so evil is that there are billions of sinful natures having full sway in people's lives. "Do not love the world or anything in the world. If anyone loves the world, the love of the Father is not in him. For everything in the world—the cravings of sinful man, the lust of his eyes and the boasting of what he has and does—comes not from the Father but from the world. The world and its desires pass away, but the man who does the will of God lives forever" (1 John 2:15-17).

What if I Fall?

If you fall, talk to the Lord about it, confess your sin, know that He forgives you, believe His blood covers you, then GET UP AND KEEP WALKING, NEVER LOOKING BACK!

It is true that Christ is able to keep us from falling (Jude 24). It is also true that He is willing to forgive and restore us if we fall into sin.

Here is His ideal for us: "My dear children, I write this to you so that you will not sin" (1 John 2:1).

Here is His provision: "But if anybody *does* sin, we have one who speaks to the Father in our defense—Jesus Christ, the Righteous One. He is the atoning sacrifice for our sins, and not only for ours but also for the sins of the whole world" (1 John 2:1, 2).

Becoming a Christian does not automatically mean that you will never sin again. In fact, I have never known a single Christian who has not sinned after baptism. But when a person receives Christ, there is a change of direction in the life. New desires spring up, new habits replace old. A new person is being created.

This much I can tell you: If you are focusing on Christ and His righteousness on a daily basis, you will sin less and less. Others will notice a change in you, although they won't be able to put their finger on it. They may ask you what's up, and this will give you an opportunity to point them to the One responsible for the change.

Victory in Jesus

When Jesus was dying upon the cross, it appeared to those assembled to be a scene of defeat. All alone, suffering so, His face disfigured from the blood mingled with tears, the Messiah did not seem to be very kingly. Satan and his demons were close at hand, inciting the crowd to hurl insults at Him. Yes, the enemy of our souls felt triumphant that day. Little did he know that he was witnessing his own demise.

"And having disarmed the powers and authorities, he made a public spectacle of them, triumphing over them by the cross" (Colossians 2:15). LOOK WHO'S TRIUMPHANT! JESUS has DISARMED the power of Satan, and made a laughing stock out of him. There is indeed POWER IN THE BLOOD! There are two things that Satan cannot do, concerning you: (1) He cannot take away your eternal life, and, (2) He cannot force you to sin.

"His divine power has given us everything we need for life and godliness through our knowledge of him who called us by his own glory and goodness. Through these he has given us his very great and precious promises, so that through them you may participate in the divine nature and escape the corruption in the world caused by evil desires" (2 Peter 1:3, 4).

That's Christ's divine power! All of our personal, physical, social, intellectual, and spiritual needs will be provided for. These are the areas that "life" and "godliness" encompass. *All of life is a gift!*

The gift is received through *knowing* Christ, in a daily, personal way. And then Peter talks about the "VERY GREAT AND PRECIOUS PROMISES" of God. There are over 800 of them in the Bible, spanning the scope of human existence. There is great power in each of these promises. By faith we release this power of God into our lives.

Peter says that through these promises we can "participate in the divine nature and escape the corruption in the world caused by evil desires." When we receive Christ as Savior and Lord, the Holy Spirit is enabled to work in our lives in a fuller way. The Bible calls it "regeneration." God's Spirit, or presence, is *within* us, and we are His *temple* (1 Corinthians 6:19; 2 Corinthians 6:16).

God's Spirit is 100% God. If God is living within you, you can indeed *participate* in the divine nature! This does not mean that you become God. It simply means that He is living out His desires in you.

But we must *walk* in the Spirit, and *be led* by the Spirit. "So I say, *live* by the Spirit, and you will not gratify the desires of the sinful nature" (Galatians 5:16). The more we submit to God's leading, the more we will be participating in His divine nature. Here is the miracle: In time, we will begin to do *naturally* what used to be totally *unnatural* for us to do. This is why I can say with all confidence to the alcoholic or the abusive husband or the chronically depressed teen, "THERE IS HOPE! LET THE LORD CHANGE YOU! LET HIM FILL YOU TO OVERFLOW-ING!"

This is what God meant when He promised, "'I will put my law in their minds and write it on their hearts'" (Jeremiah 31:33). God's law of Ten Commandments, found in Exodus chapter 20, describe what God is like. But they also point out sin. That's why it is utterly impossible for the unrenewed heart to even *want* to obey them, let alone be *able* to obey them.

God the Worker

That is why God takes the initiative in our *walk* as well as in our *birth*. He decided to write His holy principles on our hearts. Look at this promise: "For it is God who works in you to WILL and to ACT according to His good purpose" (Philippians 2:13).

GOD IS THE ONE WHO WORKS! He takes you where you are, no matter how lost or hopeless your case may be. Then He gives you the *will* to do what's right, because you don't have it naturally. This means your *desires* start lining up with *His*, without much effort on your part.

Then He gives you the *follow-through*, to *act* on those desires. This is extremely important, because *desiring* something does not make it *happen*. God is working in us, through the presence of His Spirit, to give us both the will to live for Him, and the ability to do so.

Chapter 7

A LESSON FROM GORILLAS

I remember watching a nature documentary on gorillas. It was fascinating. The focus was mainly on the mountain gorillas of Africa. I knew that gorillas were on the endangered list, but I didn't know that they were almost extinct.

In the documentary, scientists were engaged in trying to increase the number of gorillas in captivity, without taking any more animals from the wild. They were trying to create the optimum environment in which these gorillas could grow and prosper. They were somewhat successful at getting them to breed, and they provided support for expectant gorillas.

At times, unfortunately, the natural parents of a baby gorilla were dysfunctional, and were not able to care for the young one. In those cases the scientists themselves would care for the baby, and raise it through toddler stage. Then they would reintroduce the youngster back into its clan.

The scientists provided protection and security for the young gorillas as they adjusted socially. Though the process was painstaking and slow, the caretakers would spur the gorillas on, pointing them in the right direction.

Humans: An Endangered Species

"Be self-controlled and alert. Your enemy the devil prowls around like a roaring lion looking for someone to devour" (1 Peter 5:8). It's a *war* out there! I don't mean just battles in foreign lands and street violence, as bad as they are. In *this* war, you cannot see the enemy.

"For our struggle is not against flesh and blood, but against the rulers, against the authorities, against the powers of this dark world and against the spiritual forces of evil in the heavenly realms" (Ephesians 6:12).

The devil is the author of destruction, and if he had it his way, the entire world would be destroyed along with him. You see, he knows that his end is near; the lake of fire is reserved for him. And he wants to take as many humans with him as possible—just for the hate of it. He hates God and he hates God's creations. He even hates himself, but would never admit it. Instead he transfers that self-hate by striking out at the inhabitants of this world, and causing them to hate themselves also.

Satan has the majority of the world's population in his grip. Men and women behave in the most depraved manner. Just *look* at the world! Members of the same race, class, and neighborhood kill each other off. They are enslaved by the devil, and they don't even know it.

Others go through life collecting things. They collect cars and homes and degrees and spouses—they live for the moment and do whatever feels good at that moment. They embezzle and cheat and lie and feed their fantasies. They are enslaved by the devil, and they don't even know it.

Teens are inundated by music that comes straight from hell. They go to concerts to hear the demons sing. They put things in their noses and veins and lungs and wipe out their memories and shoot their parents. They are pillaged by that which turns them on, and they choose all of this because nobody has ever loved them. They are enslaved by the devil, and they don't even know it.

Poverty. Spiritual poverty. Well, my friend, you may never have an overabundance of cash, but if you follow the Lord Jesus Christ, you will live a prosperous life. You will come to the end of your days, *rich; spiritually rich.* You will have been saved from that distorter of all truth, that hideous murderer of souls, that fallen angel who doesn't even deserve to have his name on this page.

A Company of Angels

Angels. *Good* angels. Billions of them. And they aren't afraid to *fight!* Although it isn't the most important thing, it is encouraging to know that there are twice as many holy angels than fallen angels, or demons. If you are a person who finds consolation in numbers, this should help you. Just remember, though, that even *one* angel who has the power of GOD ALMIGHTY on his side, is *more than a match* for a whole legion of demons.

The strength and majesty of God cannot be matched anywhere in this universe. When the name of Jesus is invoked by one of His disciples, the powers of darkness become helpless, because a company of angels comes to the rescue of that disciple. "For he will command his angels concerning you to guard you in all your ways" (Psalm 91:11). Besides, demons don't like to be where Jesus is loved or praised. They hate spiritual songs, and they hate it when people pray, because PRAYER BRINGS GOD INTO THE ROOM!

"Are not all angels ministering spirits sent to serve those who will inherit salvation?" (Hebrews 1:14). They certainly are. God's angels help us in numerous ways—many of which we will be told about when we get to heaven.

Just as demons tempt us with evil thoughts, God's angels instruct and guide us with *good* thoughts. Most people don't know about this. We need to be aware of it, so we can listen for those timely words of wisdom. By the grace of God, it is possible to distinguish between evil and holy promptings. We can tell what comes from heaven and what comes from hell.

Just as those scientists took care of the gorillas, the angels provide *support* for us. Many people today either were raised in a *dysfunctional family* or are presently in one. Satan hates families, and is very successful at breaking them up or messing them up. The angels work to promote an *optimum environment* for growth in our households. They encourage a healthy lifestyle, firm but fair discipline of children, an atmosphere of affirmation rather than degradation, and a regular time for family worship.

As has been mentioned, the angels provide *protection* and *security* for disciples, just as the scientists protected the gorillas, especially the *young* gorillas.

Although the process is *painstaking and slow,* the angels watch over us as we bring our old lives to an end, and are born again in Christ. They know that our reintroduction into a world that is foreign to us can be full of challenges. So they *spur us on, point us in the right direction,* and *train* us not only to survive in this world, but to change it for the good.

Put on Your Armor

But angels are not the only means God has for ensuring our spiritual stability in this spiritual war. We are not merely spectators in this war; we are participants. And since "our struggle is not against flesh and blood," Paul tells us about some of the measures we can take to protect ourselves:

"Finally, be strong in the Lord and in his mighty power. Put on the full armor of God so that you can take your stand against the devil's schemes. . . . Stand firm then, with the belt of truth buckled around your waist, with the breastplate of righteousness in place, and with your feet fitted with the readiness that comes from the gospel of peace. In addition to all this, take up the shield of faith, with which you can extinguish all the flaming arrows of the evil one. Take the helmet of salvation and the sword of the Spirit, which is the word of God" (Ephesians 6:10, 11, 14-17).

Let's take a look at each of these pieces of spiritual armor. First we have the **belt of truth.** Jesus Christ *is* the truth (John 14:6). The Bible testifies of Christ, and is full of truth (2 Timothy 2:15). "'If you hold to my teaching, you are really my disciples. Then you will know the truth, and the truth will set you free" (John 8:31, 32). It is freedom that the world needs; freedom born of truth.

It should not be surprising that the devil does not want you or me to study God's Word. He knows that it contains truth and leads people to Christ. As for Satan, he is the "father of lies" (John 8:44), and he mixes a little bit of error with a whole bunch of truth, and tries to get us to swallow it. Especially in these last days, we need to study the Bible for ourselves, not taking anybody's word for it. Here is how people miss out on eternal life: "They perish because they refused to love the truth and so be saved" (2 Thessalonians 2:10).

On the personal side, we should not let falsehood reign in our lives. We should be truthful in our relationships, jobs, and everything we do. Let truth be alive in every part of your life, just as a belt goes all the way around the body.

The **breastplate of righteousness** protects the vital organs, therefore it is of utmost importance. Spiritually, our very lives depend on this piece of armor. Our own righteousnesses are like "filthy rags" (Isaiah 64:6); that is to say, we do not *have* any righteousness aside from Christ. Jesus is called "The Lord Our Righteousness" (Jeremiah 23:6). He *is* our righteousness.

There is the righteousness that we *are*, since we have accepted Christ's death in place of our own, and are freely forgiven on that basis. This is *imputed* righteousness, or *justification* (just-if-I'd-never-sinned). And there is the righteousness that we *become*, since the Holy Spirit is developing His fruit in us on a daily basis. This is *imparted* righteousness or *sanctification*, and involves lifelong character development.

Whether imputed or imparted, our righteousness is a *derived* righteousness. We receive it as a gift. The reason why this piece of armor is so important is that the devil will try to get us onto one of two extremes: (1) the position where we feel guilty all the time and do not believe that God hears us or accepts us; or, (2) the position where we become self-righteous and believe we can do no wrong, looking down on everyone else. Both positions are extremely dangerous, and the only way we will have balance is by *daily* accepting and uplifting Jesus Christ and *His* righteousness.

The **shoes of peace** are foundational in the Christian walk. Without peace, we cannot be productive disciples who in turn make disciples of the people God has placed in our lives. The world searches in vain for a lasting peace, but it cannot be found outside of a relationship with Christ. "For he himself is our peace." "Peace I leave with you; my peace I give you. I do not give to you as the world gives. Do not let your hearts be troubled and do not be afraid" (Ephesians 2:14; John 14:27).

The **shield of faith** can extinguish all the flaming arrows of the evil one. There is a good reason for this. It is because the shield is *Christ Himself.* "But you are a shield around me, O Lord, my Glorious One, who lifts up my head" (Psalm 3:3). The shield represents the presence of God in our lives.

God allows the enemy to shoot his flaming arrows at us, because this will test our faith, and give us opportunities to trust in Him. A faith that is tested becomes strong. Although the arrows actually hit the shield (trials are a real part of life), they are *extinguished;* they will only affect us in accordance with God's purpose for us.

The **helmet of salvation** protects the head or the *mind.* Satan actually controls the minds of many in this world. He seeks to do this because the mind is the control center of the person. The will, the plans, the dreams, the thoughts all reside there. Look at what the Bible has to say about our minds before we come to Christ:

"Once you were alienated from God and were enemies in your minds because of your evil behavior." "The mind of sinful man is death, but the mind controlled by the Spirit is life and peace; the sinful mind is hostile to God. It does not submit to God's law, nor can it do so" (Colossians 1:21; Romans 8:6, 7).

But when we accept Jesus Christ and His Spirit to work in our lives, we are presented with choices every day. "Therefore, I urge you, brothers, in view of God's mercy, to offer your bodies as living sacrifices, holy and pleasing to God—which is your spiritual worship. Do not conform any longer to the pattern of this world, but be transformed by the *renewing of your mind*. Then you will be able to test and approve what God's will is—his good, pleasing and perfect will" (Romans 12:1, 2).

It is Christ who renews our minds. He *is* our salvation (Psalm 27:1; Acts 4:12). By beholding Him, we become like Him. Our thoughts start resembling His thoughts. A new love springs up in us and overflows into other lives. A new joy fill our hearts. In short, our minds are *changed*.

Since there is a battle going on for our minds, how do we know if something is beneficial or dangerous? In other words, how do we know what belongs in our lives and what doesn't?

It may seem simple, but here is what I do when I'm just not sure about something. First, I ask myself if this particular event or movie or song or activity, etc., will negatively impact my relationship with Jesus. In other words, do I think Jesus would feel comfortable doing this or listening to this with me. That usually will do it.

But if I still am not sure, I shine what I call "God's Flashlight" on the activity in question. Here it is: "Finally, brothers, whatever is true, whatever is *noble*, whatever is *right*, whatever is *pure*, whatever is *lovely*, whatever is *admirable*—if anything is *excellent* or *praiseworthy*—THINK *about such things"* (Philippians 4:8). Just shine God's Flashlight on in, and if it doesn't pass the test, get rid of it.

The **sword of the Spirit** is none other than the Word of God. This, by the way, is the only *offensive* piece of armor that is listed. Many have the idea that Christians are pansies and live their lives passively. Nothing could be further from the truth! For one thing, I'd like to introduce you to my friend Willie. He's 6 foot 3, 230 pounds, and he used to be a forward in basketball and a safety in football. He's aggressively engaged in winning people to Christ (he *invites* them, naturally).

"The word of God is living and active. Sharper than any double-edged sword, it penetrates even to dividing soul and spirit, joints and marrow; it judges the thoughts and attitudes of the heart" (Hebrews 4:12). We're talking powerful print. The Bible contains words of life, and the Christian would be wise to take them with him wherever he goes, if not literally, then at least in his head, memorized.

Jesus my Lord used this sword on the devil, *successfully!* If it was good enough for Him, it's good enough for me. Three times Satan tempted Christ in the wilderness. And three times Christ replied, *"It is written. . . . ,"* and He proceeded to quote the Bible (see Luke 4:1-13).

The weapons we Christians fight with are definitely not passive: "The weapons we fight with are not the weapons of the world. On the contrary, they have divine power to demolish strongholds. We demolish arguments and every pretension that sets itself up against the knowledge of God, and we take captive every thought to make it obedient to Christ" (2 Corinthians 10:5). Before you leave your home each day, make sure you have your sword, because in between the flaming arrows, you can indeed *strike.*

How do you put the armor of God on? Notice that Paul ends his discussion on spiritual armor with a word about prayer: "And pray in the Spirit on all occasions with all kinds of prayers and requests. With this in mind, be alert and always keep on praying for all the saints" (Ephesians 6:18).

We put the armor of God on through prayer. Remember that Jesus Christ *is* our *truth, righteousness, peace, faith, salvation,* and the *Word of God.* In prayer, we ask Him to cover us with these pieces of armor. But in essence, He is covering us with *Himself.* "Clothe yourselves with the Lord Jesus Christ, and do not think about how to gratify the desires of the sinful nature" (Romans 13:14).

God the Intervener

There is one major breakdown in the gorilla analogy. The scientists learned that human intervention sometimes distorts nature's intent. The gorillas did not become all that they could become under their care, although they were fed well and treated fairly.

But when God intervenes in our lives, bringing to us the Good News of His gospel and transforming our lives, we are freed to become all that we were meant to be. Whereas before we were blinded by sin and rebellion, now we can experience the *abundant life* that God has waiting for us. *His* intervention *heightens* the quality of life, as we shall see.

Chapter 8

A PLAN IN SEARCH
OF A PERSON

God's salvation is *premeditated*. He wanted to save you long ago, before you were born, and before you became a runner. His plan of salvation was in search of you, and hopefully now has found you. But if indeed you have accepted God's gracious plan, there is something you need to know.

Saved for a Reason

You have been saved for a reason. There is purpose in God's plan for you! Everything God does is *intentional;* He doesn't make mistakes when He creates, or when He *re*-creates. Therefore you cannot possibly be a second-class person or a mistake. There is a bright future, a meaningful life, a tailor-made plan in store for you. How do I know?

Right after Paul discusses the foundational Christian doctrine that we are saved by grace through faith, he concludes with this incredible statement: "For we are God's workmanship, created in Christ Jesus to do good works, **which God prepared in advance for us to do**" (Ephesians 2:10).

When the importance of this verse finally sank in a couple of years ago, I was overwhelmed. My life hasn't been quite the same since. I went to my knees and asked God to show me those "good works" that I was meant to do in this life. I didn't want to miss out on any of them. His plan has been unfolding ever since.

Can you see the possibilities that exist for you? For just a moment, dream as big as you can. What would you really like to do with your life? What would you like to be? What would you like to accomplish, if given the chance? Now, take that dream and give it to God. Watch what He does with it.

He just may give it to you! Or He may alter it in certain ways. Or the timing may be different than you had thought. Or it just may be that God has something much different, much *bigger* in mind for you. The point is, *God has a plan for your life,* whether you are 16 or 67. And your happiness and fulfillment depend on the extent to which you are willing to follow that plan.

There are people to reach for Jesus that only you will be able to reach. And there are things to accomplish in this world that only you will be able to accomplish. These people and these things are waiting for you. What will you do about it?

Discovering Your Spiritual Gifts

The first step to understanding God's plan for your life is becoming a disciple of Christ. The second step is discovering the spiritual gift or gifts with which God has equipped you. This is the Lord's chosen means of working out His plan in your life.

We are not born with spiritual gifts. They are given to us at our conversion, when we accept Christ as Savior and Lord. Spiritual gifts are not to be confused with natural talents, which everybody has. Sometimes a spiritual gift may encompass a natural talent or two, but that is not always the case. What we need to do is discover which of the gifts we have been given, and then use our talents and opportunities to enhance those gifts.

The main thing to remember is that we do not choose which gifts we are to have; the Holy Spirit does. They are not "gifts of James or Sally." They are "gifts of the *Spirit*." "All these are the work of one and the same Spirit, and *he gives them* to each one, just *as he determines*" (1 Corinthians 12:11).

There are three main lists of spiritual gifts in the Bible, found in three important chapters: Romans 12, 1 Corinthians 12, and Ephesians 4. Some of the gifts are duplicated, and some are in only one chapter. Here is a list of the 20 gifts that are found in these three chapters:

1. Prophecy (speaking for God or foretelling the future)
2. Service
3. Teaching
4. Exhortation (strengthening the faith of others, encouraging)
5. Giving
6. Leadership
7. Mercy
8. Wisdom
9. Knowledge
10. Faith
11. Healing
12. Miracles
13. Discerning of spirits (discrimination between divine, human and satanic)
14. Tongues (speaking in languages you have not learned)

15. Interpretation of tongues
16. Apostle
17. Helps
18. Administration
19. Evangelist
20. Pastor (shepherd of people, care-giver)

Church growth specialist C. Peter Wagner points out that since none of the lists in these three chapters are complete in themselves, we can probably assume that the three lists together are not complete. By way of example, Dr. Wagner adds five more gifts that are found elsewhere in the New Testament:*

21. Celibacy
22. Voluntary poverty
23. Martyrdom
24. Hospitality
25. Missionary

How do you find out which gift or gifts you have been given? First, pray about it. Ask the Lord to show you. Then I would suggest that you complete one of several existing spiritual gift surveys.** This will give you an idea at least of how the Spirit has engifted you. Then *experiment*. For

---

*See Wagner's *Your Spiritual Gifts Can Help Your Church Grow* (Ventura, CA: Regal Books, 1979), p. 62. Available at your local Christian bookstore.

**For instance, C. Peter Wagner, *Wagner-Modified Houts Questionnaire,* rev. ed. (Pasadena, CA: Charles E. Fuller Inst. of Evangelism and Church Growth, 1985). To order, call 1-800-235-2222, and ask for the bookstore.

least of how the Spirit has engifted you. Then *experiment*. For instance, if you think you have the gift of evangelism, preach a few evangelistic sermons to the public. Take note of how comfortable you feel doing it, the response of the listeners, and what your fellow church members say. Your gift needs to be confirmed by the church, which is Christ's "body."

Remember that these gifts are given in a marked manner. For instance, every Christian should practice hospitality. But the person with the *gift* of hospitality will almost always have a new face in his or her home. This person will go out of his way to invite strangers over for a meal. Also, if you have a particular gift, you will not only derive a deep sense of fulfillment and satisfaction from exercising it; you will be quite effective at doing it as well.

The Body of Christ

"Now you are the body of Christ, and each of you is a part of it." "The body is a unit, though it is made up of many parts; and though all its parts are many, they form one body. So it is with Christ. For we were all baptized by one Spirit into one body—whether Jews or Greeks, slave or free—and we were all given the one Spirit to drink" (1 Corinthians 12:27, 12, 13).

The Bible describes God's Church as the Body of Christ. It makes sense, since we disciples are all *in* Christ and He is *in* us through His Spirit. The apostle Paul discusses spiritual gifts in the context of the Body of Christ. The gifts are likened to parts of a body:

"Now the body is not made up of one part but of many. If the foot should say, 'Because I am not a hand, I do not belong to the body,' it would not for that reason cease to be part of the body. And if the ear should say, 'Because I am not an eye, I do not belong to the body,' it would not for that reason cease to be part of the body. If the whole body were an eye, where would the sense of hearing be? If the whole body were an ear, where would the sense of smell be? But in fact *God has arranged the parts in the body,* every one of them, just as He wanted them to be. If they were all one part, where would the body be? As it is, there are many parts, but one body" (1 Corinthians 12:14-20).

Paul's point is this: No matter what part of the Body we are, we are all *vital* to the health and efficiency of the Body. No matter which of the spiritual gifts you have, it is absolutely necessary to your church. We should seek to discover our spiritual gifts, and then *use them!* Don't think that somebody else's gift is better than your's. The fact is, that person would not be very successful without you, and vice verse.

You are Necessary

God has saved you *purposefully.* His plan for you involves your participation in a local church. There is no substitute for this. If you are a Christian, then my friend you have a ministry—*automatically.* And that ministry is to be discovered and used in the church.

Just before His ascension into heaven, Jesus gave His disciples the great "Gospel Commission": "Therefore go and *make disciples* of all nations, baptizing them in the name of the Father and of the Son and of the Holy Spirit, and teaching them to obey everything I have commanded you. And surely I will be with you always, to the very end of the age" (Matthew 28:19, 20).

There are three main functions of the local church: (1) to provide an atmosphere that is conducive for Christian growth; (2) to reveal to the world what God is really like; and, (3) to make disciples of every person in that community.

The church is indeed a hospital for sinners. But it is also God's chosen medium for drawing the world to Himself. You can be a part of that process, if you are offering yourself and your ministry for the advancement of the kingdom of God.

Christ needs you, the Church needs you, and the world is waiting for you to be all that He has called you to be. I pray that God will work mightily in your life, as you go forward in His plan.

Chapter 9

THE TASTE TEST

I f you have taken the words of this book seriously, and have responded favorably, then you are on your way to being the best you can be. Abundant life, *eternal* life is your's in Jesus Christ. And if I do not see you here, I will certainly see you in heaven. I look forward to sharing eternity with you.

But if you have read this far and still have not accepted Jesus as Savior and Lord, then I invite you to "taste and see that the Lord is good" (Psalm 34:8). You have nothing to lose except your sins and loneliness, and everything to gain. Won't you give the Lord a try?

Don't be afraid to challenge God. He is not offended nor intimidated by challenges. Ask Him to show you that it is true—He has a plan for *you*. Ask Him to reveal Himself to you, and He will. I can tell you exactly how He will do it, because He did it for me. He will reveal Himself to you through people, interesting "coincidences," and your very own thoughts. If you cannot ask Him into your life, then ask Him to reveal Himself to you. He will accept even that, because He loves you.

I and many others are praying for you right now, as you read. We are praying that "the God of our Lord Jesus Christ, the glorious Father, may give you the Spirit of wisdom and revelation, so that you may know him better. . . that the eyes of your heart may be enlightened in order that you may know the hope to which he has called you, the riches of his glorious inheritance in the saints, and his incomparably great power for us who believe" (Ephesians 1:17-19).

We will continue to pray for you, because we want you to experience God's salvation, and we want to see you in heaven someday. If you are not there, it will not be because God didn't go out of His way to get you there.

I don't believe that it is best to turn to Christ out of fear. However, some people will only respond to God out of this motive. Since that is the case, it is important for you to understand that according to Bible prophecy we are living in the last days of earth's history. When Jesus comes the *second* time, it will not be as a little baby lying in a manger wrapped in swaddling clothes. *This* time it will be as the King of Kings and Lord of Lords, full of dreadful power. The mountains shall crumble, the ground shall quake, and the islands shall disappear at His appearance.

If you are His disciple on that day, no harm will befall you. You'll be caught up with Him in the clouds of glory, to be with Him forever. But if you are His *enemy* on that day, you will cry out for the rocks to fall on you—to hide you from that face—those eyes that pierce the darkness, and discern the thoughts of the heart.

There are only two roles to play on that day: friend or foe. I pray that you will choose to be a friend of God today. Accept the salvation provided in Jesus Christ, and live the life He has in store for you. Don't allow yourself to settle for anything short of God's perfect plan for your life. He created you, and He knows what will make you the happiest of all.

All blessings flow from Jesus Christ. Are there legitimate needs in your life? Take them to Jesus now, and watch what He does with them. "Seek first his kingdom and his righteousness, and all these things will be given to you as well" (Matthew 6:33).

Accepting Him is accepting Life. This is square one. If you take this step, Jesus will lead you into all truth. "Then you will know the truth, and the truth will set you free" (John 8:32).

Chapter 10

DEFENDED BY THE JUDGE

W e have all heard of the Judgment Day. The mere thought brings to many minds scenes of agony and turmoil, the wrath of God, moments of holy revenge and feelings of terrible, inescapable doom. All of this, of course, can be substantiated by the Bible, and perhaps the reality of this kind of "judgment" is appropriate.

Just the other day my wife and I heard about a carjacking in which two young males yanked a woman driver from her car, but the woman got caught in the safety belt and ended up being dragged down the road. The driver, in an effort to rid himself of his unwanted passenger, swerved into a barbed-wire fence, where the woman became lodged. Then the acosters tossed the woman's infant from the vehicle.

The infant survived, but the woman died. Upon hearing this my wife said, "Now I know why there's a hell," as she has often said in the past upon hearing of other cruel and inhumane events.

There is indeed a judgment awaiting not only carjackers but also anyone else who refuses to come to the Lord in repentance, accepting the invitation of mercy that is extended to the world in Jesus Christ. But as I said before, not one of us was meant to endure hell-fire or to be forever separated from God and eternal life.

What if I told you that, as a Christian, you have the privilege of coming into judgment *beforehand?* What if I told you that NOW is the Day of Judgment, and that you have absolutely nothing to worry about?

The First Angel's Message

"Then I saw another angel flying in midair, and he had the eternal gospel to proclaim to those who live on the earth—to every nation, tribe, language and people. He said in a loud voice, 'Fear God and give him glory, because the *hour of his judgment has come.* Worship him who made the heavens, the earth, the sea and the springs of water" (Revelation 14:6, 7).

Revelation chapter 14 presents three angels proclaiming a three-fold message of warning and preparation to the world in the last days. You might call it God's last altar call. This first angel tells us that the judgment is ALREADY GOING ON! How can this be? Well, it may be a rather new idea to us, but it sure wasn't anything new to the Bible writers, nor to Jesus. In the last chapter of the Bible, Jesus proclaims, "Behold, I am coming soon! My reward is with me" (Revelation 22:12). If Jesus brings His reward with Him when He returns, then our individual cases must have already been decided beforehand.

The Bible contemplates two groups of people, which together account for every person who has ever lived. The first group are God's professed people, who repent of their sins, and whose cases are decided prior to the Second Coming of Christ. The second group are those who disregard the promptings of God's Spirit, refuse to surrender their sins to the Savior, and whose cases will come up in the heavenly court LATER ON—after the millennium—at the Great White Throne Judgment. Of these individuals it is said, "it is a dreadful thing to fall into the hands of the living God" (Hebrews 10:31).

God the Forecaster

It's the longest time prophecy in the Bible, and it's found in Daniel 8:14. Here it is: "For two thousand three hundred days; then the sanctuary shall be cleansed" (NKJV). This is what the prophet Daniel heard an angel say while in vision. He was so baffled at what he heard and saw that he was ill for several days. "I was appalled by the vision; it was beyond understanding" (Daniel 8:27).

The angel Gabriel had told Daniel "the vision of the evenings and mornings that has been given you is true, but seal up the vision, for *it concerns the distant future*" (Daniel 8:26). Then Gabriel returns in chapter 9, while Daniel is praying. He provides the still bewildered Daniel with some important added information regarding the previous vision: "Seventy weeks are determined for your people and for your holy city, to finish the transgression, to make an end of sins, to make reconciliation for iniquity, to bring in everlasting righteousness, to seal up vision and prophecy, and to anoint the Most Holy" (Daniel 9:24, NKJV).

These are 70 weeks of probation for God's people Israel. They were given time to cease their idolatry and to return to the Lord. At the end of these 70 weeks, a repentant Israel was to have the high privilege of ushering in the arrival of "Messiah the prince," as we see in the next verse.

Gabriel continues: "Know therefore and understand, that from the going forth of the command to restore and build Jerusalem until Messiah the Prince, there shall be seven weeks and sixty-two weeks" (Verse 25, NKJV). This was God's way of telling His people *in advance* just when the Messiah—the Son of God—would come on the scene! But this is not all that the Lord reveals.

Gabriel continues: "And after the sixty-two weeks Messiah shall be *cut off*, but not for himself . . . he shall confirm a covenant with many for one week; but in the middle of the week he shall bring an end to sacrifice and offering" (Verses 26 and 27, NKJV). Here God is forecasting the very year of the death of Jesus Christ! Centuries in advance, God reveals the future with pinpoint accuracy, to silence the critic, amaze the historian, and lovingly draw the sinner to Himself.

Daniel is given a panoramic view of wondrous things to come. But he is also given the *starting point* of the first vision of 2300 days, for these 70 weeks are literally "cut off" from the larger time period. The 70 weeks and the 2300 days both have the same starting point, which Gabriel explains is the "going forth of the command to restore and build Jerusalem" (Verse 25, NKJV). In Ezra 7:12-26 we find this decree. It was given by King Artaxerxes in 457 B.C. This date, then, is the starting point of the 2300 day prophecy.

One thing we will need to keep in mind is that in prophetic, probationary time **a day equals a year.** We find God using a day to stand for a year in other places, like Ezekiel 4:6 and Numbers 14:34. But how do we really know that God is speaking of 2300 *years* in the book of Daniel? Because it is the only rendering that makes sense!

For instance, if we took the 70 weeks literally, Jesus Christ would have begun His public ministry in 456 or 455 B.C.! This, of course, is crazy. But if we apply the day-for-year rendering to the 70 weeks, the public ministry of Jesus Christ would start in the year 27 A.D., which we know to be correct from the New Testament and from history. This was the fifteenth year of Tiberius Caesar—the year of Jesus' baptism, and the commencement of His three-and-a-half years of powerful ministry (see Luke 3:1, 21).

So the 70 weeks are actually 490 years! In Daniel 9:25, the angel Gabriel explains that there would be a total of 69 weeks until Messiah the Prince. This is 483 years, from 457 B.C. to 27 A.D., when Jesus was baptized. Then Gabriel explains that "after the sixty-two weeks" the Messiah would be "cut off" or killed. (Verse 26). It is during this 70th week that Jesus is crucified on a cruel cross. In fact, as Gabriel says, it is in the "middle" of this final week that Jesus offers Himself as the spotless Lamb of God, thereby bringing the Jewish sacrificial system to an end (Verse 27). It happened just as God said it would. Exactly three-and-a-half years into His ministry, or in the middle of the 70th week, Jesus Christ was crucified. The year was 31 A.D.

Then three-and-a-half years later God's chosen people Israel came to the end of their 70 weeks of probation. In 34 A.D. the Jews stoned Stephen, as if killing the Son of God were not enough. Stephen is significant because he is the last prophet to speak to the Jewish people as the special people of God. This is what God was referring to in Daniel 9:24, "to seal up vision and *prophecy*." Stephen's speech (Acts 7) just before his death actually takes the form of the familiar Old Testament "covenant lawsuit," in which the prophet proclaims God's mighty acts on behalf of His people in the past, before stating the curses involved in breaking the covenant.

After Stephen's death, which marks the end of the 70 prophetic weeks, Paul was called to be an apostle to the Gentiles (Acts 9), and Peter was instructed that Gentiles should be accepted into the fellowship of Christ's Church (Acts 10). Thus, the Spirit of God was carefully and powerfully working out the implications of Israel's rejection of God. Now *spiritual* Israel included all who accepted Jesus Christ and became members of His Church. Let's see how all of this looks in diagram form (see figure 1).

The death of Jesus Christ was not the only thing that God forecasted. The 2300 years continue on past the 70 weeks. If you subtract 490 years from 2300 years, you are left with 1810 years, which bring us to the year 1844 A.D. This is the ending point of the 2300 years. Daniel was told that at this time the *cleansing* of the sanctuary would take place (Daniel 8:14). But what does this mean? What is a sanctuary, and how is it cleansed?

The Sanctuary

In the Old Testament, the earthly sanctuary was the place where God dwelt with His people. It was the place where the plan of redemption was portrayed in symbolic form. God said, "have them make a sanctuary for me, and I will dwell among them. Make this tabernacle and all its furnishings *exactly like the pattern* I will show you" (Exodus 25:8, 9). The Lord gave Moses a view of the *heavenly* sanctuary, and then gave him exact instructions for building the earthly sanctuary.

As you can see in figure 2, the sanctuary had an outer courtyard, a Holy Place, and a Most Holy Place. The courtyard contained the Altar of Burnt Offering and the Laver. The Holy Place contained the Table of Shewbread, the Seven Branched Candlestick, and the Altar of Incense. The Most Holy Place contained the Ark of the Covenant, which con-

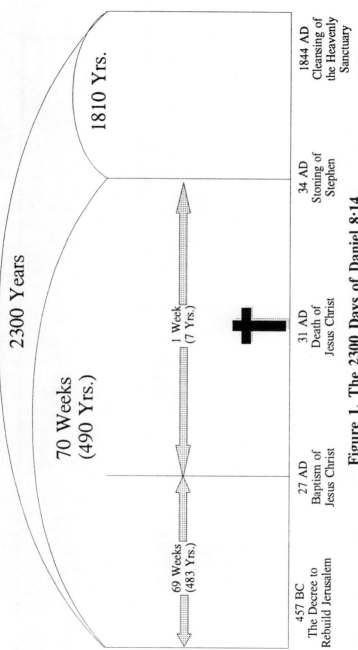

Figure 1. The 2300 Days of Daniel 8:14

2300 Years

70 Weeks (490 Yrs.)

1810 Yrs.

69 Weeks (483 Yrs.)

1 Week (7 Yrs.)

457 BC
The Decree to Rebuild Jerusalem

27 AD
Baptism of Jesus Christ

31 AD
Death of Jesus Christ

34 AD
Stoning of Stephen

1844 AD
Cleansing of the Heavenly Sanctuary

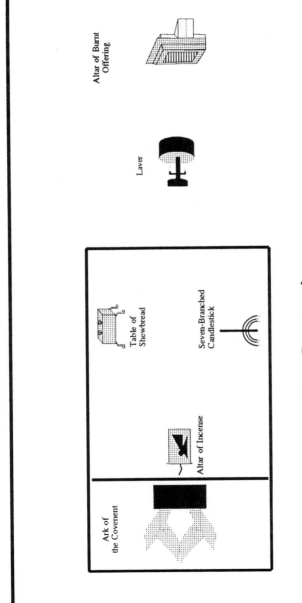

Figure 2. The Hebrew Sanctuary

tained the Ten Commandments, and upon which the glorious presence of God Almighty rested.

Jesus Christ is written all over the sanctuary! Every animal that was slain pointed forward to the true Lamb of God, who would give His life as a ransom to rescue fallen humanity. It is the blood of Jesus that cleanses us of sin, and every time a priest or an individual took the life of an innocent animal, the impression made upon the mind was vivid indeed. It was a picture of the ugliness of sin, and the lovingkindness of God. It was a picture of a God who would rather lay His life down on a cross than do away with His Holy Law, which had been broken by all. That is how seriously God takes His own commandments.

We can see this mingling of justice and mercy in the Most Holy Place. The Lord upheld His Law; the Ten Commandments were contained inside the Ark of the Covenant. But the top of the Ark was called the Mercy Seat. This is where God dwelt—right on the Mercy Seat—in between two golden angels. Yes, the Gospel can be found in the Old Testament. Here, in the Most Holy Place, we can see that God is both *just* and the *justifier* of those who have faith in Jesus (Romans 3:26).

Every priest that served in the sanctuary represented Christ as well. We must remember that Jesus is the Heavenly High Priest, who serves in the Heavenly Sanctuary. "We do have such a high priest, who sat down at the right hand of the throne of the Majesty in heaven, and who serves in the *sanctuary*, the *true tabernacle* set up by the Lord, not by man" (Hebrews 8:1, 2).

The Day of Atonement

In the earthly sanctuary system, there were daily sacrifices for sins. People by faith were freely forgiven of their sins. But the *record* of those confessed sins *remained in the sanctuary*, having been transferred daily to the sanctuary. Once a year, on the Day of Atonement, there was a special service carried out for the *cleansing* of the sanctuary. This cleansing involved a *removal* or *blotting out* of the sins that throughout the year had been transferred there.

On this holiest of all days, the Israelites were not to do any work. They were to examine themselves, and harbor an attitude of repentance before God, "because on this day atonement will be made for you, to cleanse you. Then, before the Lord, you will be clean from all you sins" (Leviticus 16:30). So, when the prophet Daniel speaks of the sanctuary being "cleansed" after 2300 years, he has in mind the Day of Atonement, which brought about a cleansing not only of the earthly sanctuary, but a very definite cleansing of the *people* as well.

Although God's people had been forgiven on a daily basis throughout the year, there was still a special time of review or "judgment" once a year in which the Lord examined whether or not the lives and attitudes of His people matched their profession. In other words, it might have been tempting for an Israelite to say in his heart, "I am a member of God's elite on this earth. I'm an Israel-ite—a son of Abraham—and I can live any way I want to live. My heritage and my membership in this chosen group will save me." But when Yom Kippur came around, that Israelite would be discovered for what he was: an unrepentant spiritual cheat.

Much the same, it might be tempting for you or me to feel rather snug in our American situation. After all, we belong to a "Christian" nation, have "In God We Trust" written on our money, and have plenty of charities to give to in order to ease our tax burdens. But the message of the Day of Atonement is that we cannot afford to be comfortable in our spiritual lethargy. THE LORD KNOWS WHO ARE HIS. It's that simple. Without a living, daily connection with Jesus Christ, we will come up empty-handed in the present judgment.

Only on the Day of Atonement did the high priest enter the Most Holy Place of the earthly sanctuary. This carries more weight when you realize that it was in the Most Holy Place where the presence of a Holy God resided. It was a solemn day of judgment—of deep searching of soul. But when it was over, there was the biggest celebration of the entire year! And so it will be for God's faithful in these last days.

Christ as Judge

In 1844, at the end of the 2300 years, Jesus Christ, the Heavenly High Priest, passed from the Holy Place into the Most Holy Place of the Heavenly Sanctuary. There He began a solemn work of investigative judgment of all who have ever professed to be His people, starting with Adam. "For it is time for judgment to begin with the *family of God*" (1 Peter 4:17). "The Lord will judge *His people*" (Hebrews 10:30). "The Judge is standing at the door!" (James 5:9).

We are given a picture of this judgment scene in the book of Daniel:

As I looked, thrones were set in place, and the Ancient of Days took his seat. His clothing was as white as snow; the hair of his head was white like wool. His throne was flaming with fire, and its wheels were all ablaze. A river of fire was flowing, coming out from before him. Thousands upon thousands attended him; ten thousand times ten thousand stood before him. *The court was seated, and the books were opened.. . . .* In my vision at night I looked, and there before me was *one like a son of man,* coming with the clouds of heaven. *He approached the Ancient of Days and was led into his presence* (Daniel 7:9, 10, 13).

This "one like a son of man" is none other than Jesus Christ, who often referred to Himself as the Son of Man (see Matthew 11:19; 16:13). The apostle John even quoted Daniel 7:13 when describing the glorified Christ as "one like a son of man" (Revelation 1:13).

What is important to notice here is that Daniel does not see this "one like a son of man" coming to this earth. Rather, He comes to the "Ancient of Days," that is, to God the Father. Therefore this is not a picture of the Second Advent of Christ, because on that day Jesus will appear with the clouds of heaven (multitudes of angels) in the atmosphere of *this earth.* This is a depiction of something other than that.

We know that it is a judgment scene because of what Daniel describes: "The court was seated, and the books were opened." We also know, based on the immediate context, that this judgment takes place during or after the time of the "little horn" (verse 8). The year 1844, then, becomes plausible contextually. We will discuss the nature and activity of this little horn in our next chapter.

The book of Daniel not only gives us a time parameter for this pre-Advent Judgment (2300 years) in chapter 8. It also gives us a beautiful description of the beginning of that event in chapter 7. This apocalyptic book, though often maligned, is actually quite consistent with itself.

This judgment is a present reality. It should be allowed to have its due impact on our daily lives—how we treat others, and the attitude of our hearts. This is not a time to play games with ourselves or with the Almighty. This is not a time to cling to our personal idols that only we know about (because Someone Else knows). This is not a time for grabbing all the gusto we can in life. "I tell you, NOW is the time of God's favor, NOW is the day of salvation" (2 Corinthians 6:2).

This judgment started with God's people who have died, and it will end with His people who are presently living. Nobody knows how far along the judgment is, but when thing is for sure: it's definitely going on! And the last time prophecy of the Bible ended in 1844. We are living in what the book of Daniel calls "the Time of the End."

Christ as Defense Attorney

The Good News is that the Judge is also our Defense Attorney! How can we lose? You see, Jesus is our High Priest, which means that He is our Mediator or Intercessor. We come to God the Father through Jesus Christ His Son. He has earned the right to represent us in the heavenly court. He pleads His very own blood on our behalf.

"Because Jesus lives forever, he has a permanent priesthood. Therefore, he is *able to save completely* those who come to God *through him,* because he always lives to *intercede* for them" (Hebrews 7:24, 25). "For Christ did not enter a man-made sanctuary that was only a copy of the true one; he entered heaven itself, *now to appear for us in God's presence*" (Hebrews 9:24).

There is nothing to fear in the judgment now taking place. We are IN CHRIST, and He is in the Holy of Holies ministering on our behalf. Christ is our Righteous Judge, and He is our Faithful Defender. Satan's role is that of Prosecutor. His very name means "one who accuses." But if you find that you have fallen into sin, my friend, even in this time of judgment, remember that in the earthly Day of Atonement the *daily sacrifices* were still carried out. So too in the *heavenly* Day of Atonement in which we find ourselves. The blood of Jesus Christ is still available to cleanse us of our sins, while we are being judged. Remember that.

What a glorious, magnificent Savior we serve! What kind of love would stoop so low to scoop us up from the gutter of depravity? I tell you, it is an amazing, other-worldly love. There is nothing like it on the face of this earth. All other loves pale in comparison.

So there is assurance in the judgment. My friend, consider the lateness of the times; let it radically impact everything you do. But also remember that Jesus is your Friend in High Places. "Therefore, since we have a great high priest who has gone through the heavens, Jesus the Son of God, let us *hold firmly to the faith* we profess. For we do not have a high priest who is unable to sympathize with our weaknesses, but we have one who has been tempted in every way, just as we are—yet was without sin. Let us then approach the throne of grace with *confidence,* so that we may receive mercy and find grace to help us in our time of need" (Hebrews 4:14-16).

The Saints Victorious

God's people have always been attacked by the enemy Satan. His accusations have been continual and his wicked scheming has been tireless. But in the current judgment, Satan will lose big.

> I was watching, and the same [little] horn was making war against the saints, and prevailing against them, until the Ancient of Days came, and a *judgment was made in favor of the saints of the Most High*, and the time came for the saints to possess the kingdom (Daniel 7:21, 22, NKJV).

Though accosted, accused, and seemingly defeated, the people of God will emerge victorious, and will be welcomed to their new home in the Father's kingdom! Their lives have been hidden in Christ—His blood has cleansed them, His righteousness has covered them, and His power has saved them. They belong with their Lord; and no accusation, however true, can keep them from their inheritance which has been purchased with the very blood of the Son of God.

Friend, if you are in Christ, judgment is not something to be afraid of. Rather, judgment is a powerful, positive verdict rendered on your behalf! I pray that you will avail yourself of the grace that Jesus holds out to you. To receive Him is to receive pardon and eternal life. Then you will see yourself in Scripture, for you will be among those "saints of the Most High," in whose favor judgment was made.

Chapter 11

WHAT'S IN A DAY?

I t was the sixth day of Creation, and the first day of
life for Adam and Eve. Everything was brand new.
As they walked together in the beautiful Garden of
Eden, they could smell the sweet fragrance of newly-formed
flowers that basked in the warmth of the sun. The trees lifted
their branches heavenward in adoration, and tiny birds
fluttered here and there, raising a song of gladness to the
sky. All of nature resounded with praise and thankful celebration. God the Father, God the Son, and God the Holy
Spirit had finished creating the heavens and the earth. All
was well.

"And on the seventh day God ended His work which
He had done, and He rested on the seventh day from all His
work which He had done. Then God blessed the seventh
day and sanctified it, because in it He rested from all His
work which God had created and made." (Genesis 2:3, 3,
NKJV.)

Why did God bless the seventh day? Why did He rest on
the seventh day? Was He tired? I don't think so. The
Sabbath was to be a perpetual memorial of Creation. In fact,
if the Sabbath had always been observed, there would never
have arisen an evolutionary theory, which claims that we
originated from chance circumstances in the form of tiny
organisms, and then through millions of years developed

into what we are today. How unlikely! How absurd! And yet it is taught in our schools as a *fact*.

Australian scientist Michael Denton, in his *Evolution: A Theory in Crisis*, expresses the pervasiveness of evolutionary thought, as well as its meaninglessness:

> The entire scientific ethos and philosophy of modern western man is based to a large extent upon the central claim of Darwinian theory that humanity was not born by the creative intentions of a deity but by a completely mindless trial and error selection of random molecular patterns.*

Life is not intentional. It is mindless; it is random. This is not only the conclusion of Darwinism. It is also its foundation. While Denton repeatedly dismisses Creation as the great myth of the ages, he also has grown increasingly critical of the theory which he espouses:

> One might have expected that a theory of such cardinal importance, a theory that literally changed the world, would have been something more than metaphysics, something more than a myth. Ultimately the Darwinian theory of evolution is no more nor less than the great cosmogenic myth of the twentieth century.**

It is not only evolutionists who are questioning their theory. Phillip E. Johnson, a law professor at the University of California at Berkeley, and former law clerk for Chief

---

* Michael Denton, *Evolution: A Theory in Crisis* (Bethesda, MD: Adler & Adler, Publishers, Inc., 1986), p. 357.

** Ibid., p. 358.

Justice Earl Warren, has taken a few swipes at evolution himself. Here he confronts Darwin's idea of "descent with modification, " which tried to account for the development of species by saying that all animals had common ancestors which were linked to their descendants by long chains of transitional intermediates:

> If common ancestors and chains of linking interme- diates once existed, fossil studies should be able, at least in some cases, to identify them. If it is possible for a single ancestral species to change by natural processes into such different forms as a shark, a frog, a snake, a penguin, and a monkey, then laboratory science should be able to discover the mechanism of change. If laboratory science cannot establish a mechanism, and if fossil studies cannot find the common ancestors and transitional links, then Darwinism fails as an empirical theory.*

Ariel Roth is a zoologist and director of the Geoscience Research Institute at Loma Linda, California. His research has been funded, at times, by the National Institute of Health, the Atomic Energy Commission, and other entities. In a recent interview, Roth was asked whey he believed in a relatively young earth (under 10,000 years old). Here is what he said:

> If this earth is 3.5 million years old, then at present rates of sedimentation, all the oceans would have filled up with sediments 19 times over. At current

---

* Phillip E. Johnson, *Darwin on Trial* (Downers Grove, IL: InterVarsity Press, 1991), p. 66.

rates of erosion the continents would have eroded away several hundreds of times!*

When asked what other evidences he considered stronger for Creation, Roth summarized:

There's the problem of accounting for the beginnings of life without intelligent design and effort—which creationists identify with God. Also, there are serious gaps in the fossil record, and missing strata in the earth's crust, that have proved most difficult for the evolutionary model.**

The seventh-day Sabbath points us to a Creator-God, who does everything intentionally and with style. We are amazing, we humans. And not one of us is a clone! All of these systems running smoothly and constantly inside of us without any effort on our part. Don't tell me it all just "happened." The Sabbath reminds us that there is a God in heaven who is to be worshipped because He created all things.

It should not surprise us that God chose something in the realm of time to regularly focus our attention and adoration. Time is the one thing that we can do absolutely nothing about. We all stand helpless in the face of time. That is the point.

God knew that time was a realm beyond our control, so He chose to commune with us during a piece of time—called the Sabbath—to draw our minds into a deeper

---

* Richard H. Utt, "The Working Model Doesn't Work," *Liberty* (March/April, 1993), p. 14.

** Ibid.

acknowledgment of His lordship. The Sabbath was instituted as an eternal reminder that we did not *create* ourselves,
and we cannot *save* ourselves. It is a picture of grace.

For six days God worked. Adam and Eve's first full day
was the Sabbath. They had nothing to offer God except their
praise and thanksgiving. They joyfully celebrated the gift of
life, and openly communed with their Father. For six days
God worked; and then He rested. And we would do well to
do likewise.

The Sabbath is a breath of fresh air in today's atmosphere of pressure, deadlines, self-centeredness, and intense
competition. For six days we manipulate, exert our influence, scheme, and somehow try to make the most of our
time. But on the *seventh* day, God exerts *His* influence upon
us. We allow ourselves to be enamored with Him; to be
caught up in *His* love, *His* fellowship, *His* truth, and *His* joy.

After the Fall

After Adam and Eve fell into sin the entire world was
drastically altered. Sin touched every part of God's creation.
The vegetation began to show signs of decay, and animals
began to prey on one another. As time passed, the human
race gradually forgot about the Sabbath. Men and women
worshipped gods of stone and wood, and perverted their
natural sexual inclinations. Many centuries passed, and
when God miraculously rescued His people Israel from
Egyptian bondage, they too had forgotten about the
Sabbath.

This is why God had to *remind* them of it when He gave
them the Ten Commandments. On Mount Sinai He uttered
these words:

Remember the Sabbath day by keeping it holy. Six
days you shall labor and do all your work, but the

seventh day is a Sabbath to the Lord your God. On it you shall not do any work, neither you, nor your son or daughter, nor your manservant or maidservant, nor your animals, nor the alien within your gates. For in six days the Lord made the heavens and the earth, the sea, and all that is in them, but he rested on the seventh day. Therefore the Lord blessed the Sabbath day and made it holy. (Exodus 20:8-11).

The Sabbath was so important that the Lord made it the fourth commandment. God's Ten Commandments were meant to be eternal. They were not meant to be changed or tampered with by anyone. Every good and descent law in history has had God's Law at its foundation.

But why is it that hardly anyone keeps the seventh-day Sabbath nowadays? Why is it that most Christians worship on Sunday, the *first* day of the week? We will be answering this question in this chapter. But first, let's find out which day Jesus observed. After all, the disciple should be concerned about following his Master's example.

The Lord of the Sabbath

"He went to Nazareth, where he had been brought up, and on the Sabbath day he went into the synagogue, as was his custom" (Luke 4:16). Jesus' custom was to observe the seventh-day Sabbath. This should not surprise us. In Old Testament times, He had a special day, as we have seen (see also Isaiah 58:13). Since Christ never changes, why would He have a different day in the New Testament?

In fact, Jesus tells us which day is His special day. "For the Son of Man is Lord of the Sabbath" (Matthew 12:8). The Sabbath is indeed the Lord's Day. Many people teach that Christ did away with the Law. But is this the case? Did Jesus come to this earth to *abolish* His Law, or to *magnify* it? Let's let Him answer that:

"Do not think that I have come to abolish the Law or the Prophets; I have not come to abolish them but to *fulfill* them. I tell you the truth, until heaven and earth disappear, not the smallest letter, not the least stroke of a pen, will by any means disappear from the Law until everything is accomplished" (Matthew 5:17, 18). One gets the feeling that God's Law is here to stay.

Jesus could have easily done away with the Law. But instead He goes on to illustrate what it truly means to "keep" the commandments. He says that murder is not merely something criminals do with guns; it's the hatred we harbor in our hearts towards our neighbors. Adultery is not merely having an affair; it's the lust within us that no one sees. Keeping the Sabbath involves not merely resting; it is a time for ministering to the needs of others. What is Jesus saying? That God's Law is deeper and broader than we think.

In His daily association with people, we see Jesus living His own Law. He practiced what He had previously engraved in stone. You might say that the Law was personified in Him. In the way He related to His Father, and in the way He treated those with whom He came in contact, we can see just how Jesus "fulfilled" the Law: He perfectly *obeyed* it. You can "fulfill" a law as many times as you like. But your fulfilling of it does not do away with it. The law is still there to be fulfilled again.

When you think about it, if the Law could simply be put aside, why did Jesus have to lay down His life? Why go through all that hassle and heartache if the Law was just a passing thing? Rather, Jesus died in order to *uphold* the Law, and to save you and me—the sinners who have broken it.

There *is* something that came to an end at the cross of Christ. It is the sacrificial system, which pointed forward to the time when the true Lamb of God would be slain for the salvation of the world. This is the law that is no more, since continuing those sacrifices would be a slap in the holy face of Jesus Christ.

Is there a friction between Law and Grace? Does our faith in Christ exempt us from observing His Law? "Do we, then, nullify the law by this faith? *Not at all!* Rather, we *uphold* the law" (Romans 3:31). The Law was never meant to save anyone. Only Grace can do that. Christians get into trouble when they try to save themselves by keeping the Law, or when they disregard the Law once saved. Loving obedience is the only appropriate response for the disciple of Christ. We do not keep the Law in order to be saved; we keep it because we *are* saved.

While it is true that Christ rose from the garden tomb on the first day of the week, it is also true that He had *rested* in the tomb over the Sabbath. Even in the tomb Jesus observed His holy day! There is not a single verse in all the New Testament stating that the Sabbath has been changed from the seventh day to the first day, Sunday. You can look all you want, but you won't find it.

All of God's people in the Bible were Sabbath-keepers. The Old Testament believers kept the Sabbath, Jesus Christ kept the Sabbath, His disciples kept the Sabbath even after He died, and even Paul, the prolific promoter of "grace," kept the Sabbath (Acts 17:2). In fact, the Bible says that even on the New Earth we will be keeping the Sabbath! (Isaiah 66:23). So if Jesus didn't change the Sabbath, and the apostles didn't change it, WHO DID?

The Subtle Change

Already in Paul's day, a bad attitude concerning God's Law was beginning to surface. Paul wrote, "for the secret power of lawlessness is already at work" (2 Thessalonians 2:7). The early church was a persecuted Church. Both the Romans and the Jews despised Christians. But in time Christianity became a popular religion. And in order to appeal to the pagan masses, the church began to incorporate pagan customs and holidays.

Idols and images were brought into the churches, so the Gentile would feel more at home. Instead of a myriad of gods and goddesses, they could now worship and pray to wooden and stone images of various saints. And as the Roman church sought to distance itself from the Jews, who had put Jesus to death, it also distanced itself from the Jewish Sabbath. The pagan Day of the Sun made its way into the forefront.

At first both the Sabbath and the Sun-Day were observed. But then the Sabbath began to be associated with fasting and drudgery, while Sunday became a day of celebration, in honor of Christ's resurrection. The pagan festival came to be honored as if it had been divinely instituted. Soon the majority of Christians were observing only Sunday.

Christianity then became the state religion—fully sanctioned by the Roman government. The church at Rome had a powerful influence on the emperor. And in 321 A.D., the emperor Constantine enacted a Sunday law which made Sunday a public festival throughout the entire Roman empire, and forbade all labor on that day.

Daniel's "Little Horn"

God had predicted this as well. Long before this, the Lord had revealed to the prophet Daniel that a "little horn" power would arrive on the scene sometime in the future. This power would "try to change the set times and laws" (Daniel 7:25). The original Aramaic for "law" here is literally "divine law." To discover the identity of this little horn, we must understand God's forecast of the great world empires.

In addition to His prediction of the exact year of Christ's death, God predicted the order in which the world's great empires would arise. In Daniel 2, the Babylonian king Nebuchadnezzar has a dream. In his dream, he sees a giant image whose head is gold, chest and arms are silver, belly and thighs are bronze, legs are iron, and whose feet are partly iron and partly clay (verses 32 and 33).

Daniel interprets the king's dream, explaining that the gold represents Babylon, and that the other four sections of the great statue represent the empires which would follow Babylon in order, each conquering its predecessor (verses 36-42). From history we know these to be the empires of Medo-Persia, Greece, and Rome, and the ten Germanic tribes which successfully attacked and dismembered the Roman Empire.

Daniel 7 repeats the prediction, describing these kingdoms as "beasts." In Bible prophecy, a "beast" represents an earthly government, kingdom, or power (Daniel 7:17, 23). This time Daniel has a dream, and in his dream he sees four incredible beasts: the first a lion, the second a bear, the third a leopard, and the fourth a "dreadful and terrible, exceedingly strong" beast (verses 4-7, NKJV). It is explained to Daniel that these four beasts represent four kingdoms that would rule the earth (verse 17). Again, from history we know the identity of these kingdoms. The lion is Babylon, the bear is Medo-Persia, the leopard is Greece, and the dreadful beast is the Roman Empire.

This fourth beast has ten horns, representing ten divisions (verse 24). The Roman Empire was broken up by ten Germanic tribes by A.D. 476, when the city of Rome was sacked. A "little horn" was to uproot three of these ten divisions (verses 8, 20, 24). Daniel saw that "this horn had eyes like the eyes of a man and a mouth that spoke boastfully" (verse 8). "He will speak against the Most High and oppress his saints and try to change the set times and the laws. The saints will be handed over to him for a time, times, and half a time" (verse 25).

A "time" is another way of saying "year" (see Daniel 4:16). So for three-and-a-half years of prophetic time this little horn power would wage war against God's people (verses 21 and 25). Using the day-for-year formula, and understanding that Hebrew years contained 360 days, we can correctly interpret this "time, times, and half a time" as 1260 years:

Time	360
Times	720
Half a Time	+180
	1260

The little horn was to rise to power during the time of the ten divisions of the Roman Empire, would rule for 1260 years, and would attempt to change God's Law, including the Sabbath commandment. The book of Revelation also reveals the little horn power, using different symbolism. The "beast" of Revelation 13 and the little horn of Daniel 7 refer to the same power.

"The beast was given a mouth to utter proud words and blasphemies and to exercise his authority for forty-two months. He opened his mouth to blaspheme God, and to slander his name and his dwelling place and those who live in heaven. He was given power to make war against the saints and to conquer them. And he was given authority over every tribe, people, language and nation. All inhabitants of the earth will worship the beast—all whose names have not been written in the book of life belonging to the Lamb that was slain from the creation of the world" (Revelation 13:5-8).

How do we know that this beast is the same entity as Daniel's little horn?

1. They both rule for 1260 years (Revelation 12:6; 12:14; 13:5). Forty-two months of thirty days each equals 1260 prophetic days or years:

$$\begin{array}{r} 42 \\ \underline{\times 30} \\ 1260 \end{array}$$

2. They both have at their head a man with a "mouth" speaking words of blasphemy against God, which includes mixing paganism with Christianity, and claiming to stand in the place of God on earth.

3. They both persecute the saints of God.

Revelation adds that this beast will receive the worship of people, so we know that it is a *religious* power, as well as a secular power. So the question is, what religious/political power was coming on the scene during the break-up of the Roman Empire, persecuted God's people for 1260 years, had at its head a man who claimed to be the representative of God on earth, and attempted to change God's Law? There can be only one possible entity that fits the characteristics of Daniel's little horn and Revelation's beast. It is the Roman Catholic Church, or the Papacy.

Though in existence during the early centuries, the Papacy began a special period of supremacy in A.D. 538, after destroying, with the help of Zeno and Justinian, the three tribes of the Heruli (493), the Vandals (534), and finally the Ostrogoths (538). According to Daniel, the little horn was to "uproot" tree of the ten divisions of the Roman Empire (Daniel 7:8, 20, 24).

The Roman church continued to rule until 1798, when the Pope was taken into captivity by the French general Berthier. Revelation describes this event as the "fatal wound" that the beast was to receive (13:3). This period is exactly 1260 years, and during the Medieval Ages and following, the Papacy was in full control of all of Europe's peoples and political rulers. Millions of Christians were killed—Waldenses, Albigenses, Hugenots, followers of the Reformers, and some 40,000 during the Spanish Inquisition—because they refused to obey the dictates of the Papacy.

Remember, it is not the *people* of this church that the Bible speaks out against. There are wonderful Catholic Christians worldwide who sincerely love the Lord, as there are in every church. But the Papal *system* is what has set itself up against God Almighty and His Law. No one can ever really change God's Law. But you can sure "try." That is what the Papacy has done.

Paul, describing the "secret power of lawlessness" or "antichrist," says, "He opposes and exalts himself over everything that is called God or is worshiped, and even sets himself up in God's temple, proclaiming himself to be God" (2 Thessalonians 2:4). The Roman Catholic Church claims that the Pope is infallible, when making an official decree. The Pope's word is even placed above the Bible itself, due to an erroneous assumption that the Spirit is present in the church to modify the teachings of Scripture.

It is also taught that priests have the ability to forgive sins, which is what the phrase "sets himself up in God's temple" means. According to the Bible, GOD ALONE can forgive sins. Jesus could do it because He was God Incarnate. As our heavenly High Priest, Jesus Christ alone should hear our confessions; and He alone should say, "I absolve you." "For there is one God and one mediator between God and men, the man Christ Jesus" (1 Timothy 2:5). For a mere mortal to seek to fulfill this role in our lives is the highest form of blasphemy.

The Catholic priests also re-crucify Christ whenever they conduct a mass. When the priest pronounces the blessing on the bread and wine, it is believed and taught that these emblems actually become the very flesh and blood of Jesus Christ. So, not only does the church tamper with Christ's priestly ministry; it tampers with His *death,* too. "Christ was sacrificed *once* to take away the sins of many people" (Hebrews 9:28). No church has the right to have a monopoly on Christ's once-for-all death. How do you think this makes Jesus feel? It's as if His own sacrifice for sins in A.D. 31 wasn't good enough!

Even Martin Luther, the great leader of the Protestant Reformation, identified the Roman Catholic Church as the little horn of Daniel. This interpretation is nothing new. The problem is, most churches today have departed from their Protestant heritage by misapplying these ancient prophecies to either circumstances before Christ, or to those in the distant future. But these efforts are fruitless and are not in harmony with the continuity of biblical prophecy.

In order to have images of saints in their churches, the Papacy *removed* the second commandment, which forbids the making and worship of idols and images (see Exodus 20:4-6). Then, in order to get back to the original number ten, they *split* the tenth commandment, which prohibits the coveting of another's possessions and another's spouse, thus making two separate commandments (see Exodus 20:17). So God's Law was tampered with, just as He said it would be (Daniel 7:25).

As if this were not enough, the Roman church reinterpreted the Sabbath commandment to mean Sunday. They removed the bulk of the wording of the fourth commandment, which specifies that it is the *seventh* day that God made holy. The keeping of the first day of the week became part of tradition, which explains why so many Christians today observe it instead of the seventh-day Sabbath. During His public ministry, Jesus warned the Pharisees against altering the truth of God for the sake of convenience. He said, "You have let go of the commands of God and are holding on to the traditions of men" (Mark 7:8). "In vain they worship Me, teaching as doctrines the commandments of men" (Matthew 15:9, NKJV).

Only God can make something holy. For you or me or a church to claim to make something holy is a farce. It is usurping the role of God. The Christian should take these words of Jesus seriously: "If you love Me, keep *My* commandments" (John 14:15, NKJV).

Here is yet another way to identify the beast. Revelation 13:18 says, "Here is wisdom. Let him who has understanding calculate the number of the beast, for it is the number of a man: His number is 666" (NKJV).

It is interesting to note that the ancient Babylonian system was based on the number six. This hexamal system has been used by many nations through the centuries, until recently when most have adopted the metric system (based on 10). Here in the U.S.A. we are still on the hexamal system. Our gallon, hour, minute, mile, etc. are all based on the number six.

Revelation's "666" has been called the "Satanic trinity," since the number six has long been identified as an affront to God's kingdom, signified by the number seven, which represents completeness or perfection.

There has been much speculation about this number through the centuries. But it's really quite simple. The text says that in order to discover the number of the beast we must "calculate" or count the number of the beast. We must add it up. One of the official titles of the Pope is Vicarius Filii Dei, which means "Vicar of the Son of God." If we add up or "calculate" the numerical value of these letters, in several languages, we have exactly 666, which is the number of the beast. Here is the Latin version:

V	=	5	F	=	0	D	= 500	112
I	=	I	I	=	1	E	=	0	53
C	=	100	L	= 50		I	=	1	+501
A	=	0	I	=	1			501	666
R	=	0	I	=	1				
I	=	1			53				
V or U	=	5							
S	=	0							
		112							

The Second Angel's Message

"A second angel followed and said, 'Fallen! Fallen is Babylon the Great, which made all the nations drink the maddening wine of her adulteries'" (Revelation 14:8). Ancient Babylon attacked God's people and took them into captivity. But that is not all they did. King Belshazzar invited all of his leaders to a great feast, and while intoxicated, he called for the holy vessels which had been taken from God's temple in Jerusalem. From these vessels he and his rulers drank liquor, and offered praise to the gods of gold and silver. It was an attempt to combine the elements of the worship of the true God with the worship of pagan gods. That night Belshazzar saw God's handwriting on the wall. The message was simple and straightforward: "You have been weighed on the scales and found wanting" (Daniel 5:27). That very night Belshazzar was slain. Darius the Mede took over the kingdom.

It is this mixing of truth and error, of true and false worship, that the second angel of Revelation 14 is proclaiming.

Spiritual Babylon is guilty of spiritual adultery; of being unfaithful to God by corrupting spiritual standards. The "fall" that the angel announces is a *moral* fall. Modern Babylon has tampered with God's revealed will found in His Word, including the Ten Commandments.

The second angel says that this Babylon "made all the nations drink the maddening wine of her adulteries" (Revelation 14:8). These "adulteries" refer to the many man-made, unscriptural teachings that the Papacy has come up with through the years. Here are some examples:

1. **Devotion to Mary**: The worshipping of Mary, the mother of Jesus.

2. **Purgatory**: The teaching that there is a second chance at salvation after death.

3. **Transubstantiation:** The doctrine of the mystical presence of Christ in the bread and wine.

4. **Penance/Indulgences:** The idea that we can *work* or *pay* our way into acceptance with God.

5. **Intercession of Saints:** The teaching that the saints of old are actually alive in heaven, and can pray for us, having influence with God.

6. **Sunday Sacredness:** The transfer of sanctity from the biblical Sabbath to Sunday.

Indeed, "all the nations" have drunk their share of the wine of these adulteries. "Babylon" means "confusion," and there are an awful lot of confused people in our world today. Babylon is more than the Papacy. Babylon is apostate Christianity; and God is calling His people OUT of her. "Come out of her, my people, so that you will not share in her sins, so that you will not receive any of her plagues; for her sins are piled up to heaven, and God has remembered her crimes" (Revelation 18:4, 5).

These are serious words, because we are living in serious times. If you sense that the message of this chapter is rather blunt, remember that it is God, not me, who is warning us against remaining in a system of untruth. He, not me, is calling us out of darkness into His marvelous light (1 Peter 2:9). Revelation 14 contains God's three-fold message for this time. Are you listening, Christian?

The Third Angel's Message

"A third angel followed them and said in a loud voice: 'If anyone worships the beast and his image and receives his mark on the forehead or on the hand, he, too, will drink of the wine of God's fury, which has been poured full strength into the cup of his wrath. He will be tormented with burning sulphur in the presence of the holy angels and of the Lamb. And the smoke of their torment rises for ever and ever. There is no rest day or night for those who worship the beast and his image, or for anyone who receives the mark of his name" (Revelation 14:9-11).

This is a heavy message. I don't know about you, but I do not personally want to receive the mark of the beast. There is not a very bright future connected with it. We have already identified the beast as the Roman Catholic system. We will discuss the "image" of the beast next chapter. Let us now discover what this mark of the beast will be.

Some people think that this mark is the number 666. But we are told that this is simply the number of his name (Revelation 15:2). According to the Bible, the mark must be something that nearly all the world follows the Catholic Church in (Revelation 13:3). Therefore it cannot be the worship of saints, confession to an earthly priest, or purgatory. Many of the world's Christians do not hold to these beliefs.

So what is the mark of the beast? Here is a clue. Listen to the closing words of the third angel: "This calls for patient endurance on the part of the saints who obey God's commandments and remain faithful to Jesus" (Revelation 14:12). Evidently the mark of the beast is the opposite of God's commandments, because by keeping His commandments one will not receive the mark. What is the one commandment that the Roman Catholic Church has reinterpreted, and that nearly all the world follows after her in? You guessed it. It's the Sabbath commandment.

Listen to what Catholic leaders have said regarding Sunday:

"Ques.- Have you any other way of proving that the (Catholic) Church has power to institute festivals of precept (to command holy days)?"

"Ans.- Had she not such power, she could not have done that in which all modern religionists agree with her: she could not have substituted the observance of Sunday the first day of the week, for the observance of Saturday the seventh day, a change for which there is no Scriptural authority.

-Stephan Keenan, *A Doctrinal Catechism*, page 176.

"Protestants . . . accept Sunday rather than Saturday as the day for public worship after the Catholic Church made the change . . . But the Protestant mind does not seem to realize that . . . in observing the Sunday, they are accepting the authority of the spokesman for the church, the Pope."

-*Our Sunday Visitor*, February 5, 1950.

"The Catholic Church for over one thousand years before the existence of a Protestant, by virtue of her divine mission, changed the day from Saturday to Sunday."

-*The Catholic Mirror*, September, 1893.

"Of course the Catholic Church claims that the change was her act. . . . And the act is a MARK of her ecclesiastical authority in religious things."

-H.F. Thomas, Chancellor of Cardinal Gibbons.

The mark of the beast definitely has to do with Sunday. According to the Bible, this mark will be state-enforced (Revelation 13:16). So what is the mark of the beast? It is state-enforced Sunday observance. It may surprise you to learn that there are Sunday "Blue Laws" on the books of many of our states. There is also currently a powerful push on the part of Christian fundamentalists to make Sunday a mandated national day of rest.

People will receive the mark of the beast when governments enforce Sunday observance as a law. Those who believe this should be done will be receiving the mark in their "foreheads" (has to do with agreement and the will).

Those who just go along with it for the sake of convenience will be receiving the mark in their "right hand" (has to do with acting, but not really agreeing). This is what the Bible means by these terms.

We are told that those who refuse to receive the mark of the beast will not be able to buy or sell (Revelation 13:17). Thus, an economic boycott of a sorts will occur, and those who are faithful to God and His commandments will be the targets. Certainly it will not be the most popular thing to go against the tide in these last days. But it will be the *right* thing to do. Even though virtually the entire world will receive this dreaded mark, God will still have His faithful people who will stand up for Jesus Christ and His truth.

A Simple Test of Loyalty

The Bible gives us a look behind the scenes. There is a WAR going on! It is a war between Christ and Satan. It is an all-out attempt by the devil to usurp Christ's rightful position as Ruler, High Priest, and Law-Giver. This has always been the case (see Isaiah 14:13, 14). But it is especially the case in the last days of earth's history.

We are told that the dragon, or Satan, is the one who gives the beast "his power and his throne and great authority" (Revelation 13:2). Why is it that Satan seeks to tamper with God's Law? Why does he especially pick on the Sabbath commandment? It is because the Sabbath in these last days is called the "Seal of the Living God" (Revelation 7:2).

Right before the seven last plagues are poured out upon this world, the apostle John hears an angel cry, "Do not harm the land of the sea or the trees until we put a seal on the foreheads of the servants of our God" (Revelation 7:3). Unlike Satan's mark, you can only receive God's seal in the forehead. In other words, keeping God's Sabbath is not a matter of convenience. He wants only true, committed, believing disciples to worship Him in spirit and in truth.

It makes sense, doesn't it? The seal of God is the very opposite of the mark of the beast. A better way of saying it is that the mark of the beast is a *counterfeit* of the seal of God. It originates with a counterfeit god (Satan) and involves a counterfeit sabbath. There is God's seal, and there is Satan's mark. You will either receive one or the other in the near future.

In ancient times, a ruler's "seal" included three things: his name, his title, and his territory. The fourth commandment or Sabbath commandment contains these three elements:

Name   : **The Lord your God**
Title   : **Creator**
Territory : **The heavens and the earth**
              (Exodus 20:8-11).

Dr. Meredith Kline, in his book *Treaty of the Great King*, reveals the remarkable resemblance between God's covenant of Ten Commandments with Israel and the suzerainty (also called vassal) type of international treaty found in the ancient Near East.* Here is how he describes one of the similarities:

> As a further detail in the parallelism of external appearance it is tempting to see in the Sabbath sign

---

* Meredith G. Kline, *Treaty of the Great King: The Covenant Structure of Deuteronomy* (Grand Rapids: William B. Eerdman's, 1963).

presented in the midst of the ten words the equivalent of the suzerain's dynastic seal found in the midst of the obverse of the international treaty documents. Since in the case of the Decalogue the suzerain is Yahweh, there will be no representation of him on his seal, but the sabbath is declared to be his 'sign of the covenant' (Exodus 31:13-17).*

Dr. Kline, a Sunday-observer, honestly discusses the role of the Sabbath in the relationship between God and His people. He continues to describe the centrality of the Sabbath, perhaps without realizing that it is also Revelation's "seal of God":

By means of his sabbath-keeping, the image-bearer of God images the pattern of that divine act of creation which proclaims God's absolute sovereignty over man, and thereby he pledges his covenant consecration to his Maker. The Creator has stamped on world history the sign of the sabbath as his seal of ownership and authority.**

Is it any wonder that the devil, through human instrumentality, would want to tamper with this particular commandment? To seek to change God's holy Sabbath is to play God! It is a direct assault on God Himself! This is why there is such a serious warning against receiving the mark of the beast. To do so is to place yourself on the side of rebellion. To do so is to take part in Satan's attack on God and His truth.

---

* Ibid., p. 18.
** Ibid., pp. 18-19.

We should not be surprised that God's test of loyalty in these final days involves something as simple as a *day*. After all, the object God chose in the Garden of Eden was rather simple as well. It was tree of all things. And yet the issues surrounding that tree and its forbidden fruit were *enormous*. The failure of that simple test has had far-reaching effects on the human race. And so it is with the Sabbath/Sunday test.

You can find the month and the year in nature. These are the number of days it takes the moon to revolve around the earth, and the earth to revolve around the sun, respectively. But you won't find the seven-day week anywhere in nature. It is not arrived at by observing the stars or the seasons. Though the seven-day week makes good sense to most people, it is not logically determined; it is not based on mere human reason. Rather, God Himself instituted the week when He created this world.

Similarly, all the other nine commandments make logical sense. Even resting one day in seven has seemed like a good idea to many throughout the millennia. But the only way to know which day (and likewise which tree in the Garden) is to trust what God says, even though it cannot be scientifically proven. This is the highest test of morality—to take God at His word because He is trustworthy.

Will you, my friend, take your stand for the Lord Jesus in earth's final chapter? Will you be among those disciples "who obey God's commandments and remain faithful to Jesus"? Or will you settle for something less than God's best for your life.

Chapter 12

AMERICA'S CHANGING FACE

I n our previous chapter, we discovered that God has an extremely serious warning in these last days against worshipping the beast and receiving his mark. It is really a matter of eternal life and death. State-enforced Sunday observance was found to be this mark of the beast, in contrast to God's ordained seventh-day Sabbath. Few realize just how close to home this gets.

The Lamb-like Beast

Then I saw another beast coming up out of the earth, and he had two horns like a lamb and spoke like a dragon. And he exercises all the authority of the first beast in his presence, and causes the earth and those who dwell in it to worship the first beast, whose deadly wound was healed. He performs great signs, so that he even makes fire come down from heaven on the earth in the sight of men. And he deceives those who dwell on the earth by those signs which he was granted to do in the sight of the beast, telling those who dwell on the earth to make an image to the beast who was wounded by the sword and lived. He was granted power to give breath to the image of the beast, that the image of the beast should both speak and cause as many as would not worship the image of the beast to be killed. And he causes all, both small and great, rich and poor, free and slave, to receive a mark on their right hand or on their foreheads, and that no one may buy or sell except one who has the mark or the name of the beast, or the number of his name (Revelation 13:11-1, 17, NKJV).

Notice that this second beast rises up out of the *earth*, instead of the sea, like the first beast (see Revelation 13:1). In Bible prophecy, the "sea" represents "peoples, multitudes, nations and languages" (Revelation 17:15). So the "earth" must represent a sparsely populated area.

Notice also that this second beast *looks* like a lamb, but *speaks* like a dragon! What a description of contrast! Evidently, this power undergoes a major personality change.

Thirdly, note that this lamb-like beast "exercises all the authority of the first beast *in his presence*" (Revelation 13:12). This means that these two powers are *contemporaries*. Furthermore, this second beast comes to power just as the first beast is going into captivity (Revelation 13:10, 11). From our previous chapter, we know that the Papacy received her "deadly wound" in 1798, when Napoleon's General Berthier took the Pope captive. This was at the end of the 1260 years of Papal supremacy that the Bible foretold. So the lamb-like beast had to have arisen right around that time.

John Wesley, speaking of the two-horned beast in 1754, wrote, "He is not yet come, though he cannot be far off, for he is to appear at the end of the forty-two months of the first beast" (*Notes on Revelation*, page 427).

What nation was emerging in a sparsely populated area of the earth during the latter part of the eighteenth century? There can be no mistake. The lamb-like beast is the United States of America, whose Declaration of Independence was signed in 1776. It is the country I love. It is the land that, in an age of religious persecution, provided a haven of rest for tired pilgrims looking for freedom. This was a partial fulfill-ment of Revelation 12:16, "But the earth helped the woman [Church] by opening its mouth."

The "two horns" represent civil and religious freedom, upon which this country was founded. Our democratic form of government "of the people" has been the envy of all the world. Our religious tolerance has ensured the liberty of individual conscience. For over 200 years the U.S.A. has been a freedom-loving nation; the defender of the defense-less; a super-power with a heart. But the Bible predicts a time when America will speak as a dragon.

America is accurately described in Revelation as a pow-erful nation who "performs great signs" and "makes fire come down from heaven" (13:13, NKJV). But how will America cause all who dwell in the world to "worship the first beast" or the Papacy?

The Image of the Beast

We are told that this lamb-like beast, America, will tell the world to make an image to the first beast (verse 14). What is an image? It is a likeness of something. Remember that the Roman Catholic Church is the first beast. The Vatican is a union of church and state. It has always been. It is the only religious entity in the world that receives the ambassadors of the nations. And we have previously dis-covered that the "mark" of this beast's authority is Sunday-observance. Does it surprise you to hear that this is precisely the point in which America will "image" the Papacy?

"And he causes all, both small and great, rich and poor, free and slave, to receive a mark on their right hand or on their foreheads, and that no one may buy or sell except one who has the mark or the name of the beast, or the number of his name" (verses 16 and 17). Government-enforced Sunday observance, and an economic boycott against all who stand up for God's commandments. We're talking hard times here. It's pretty bad when it affects your dinner table!

The United States will be the ENFORCER of the mark of the beast. There will come into existence a union of church and state the likes of which have never been seen. This image of the first beast will be brought about when the laws of our land are either changed or reinterpreted to allow for a mandated observance of Sunday. And eventually, all who refuse to "worship" or abide by this new law run the risk of losing their lives (verse 15). But Jesus says, "Do not be afraid of those who kill the body but who cannot kill the soul. Rather, be afraid of the one who can destroy both soul and body in hell" (Matthew 10:28).

How will America "speak as a dragon?" This "speaking" will be the *actions* of its legislative and judicial branches. The only way that a national Sunday law could ever be enacted is if our constitutional separation of church and state should be tampered with. There is evidence that America's image of the beast is already being set up. Listen to what our current Chief Justice has to say:

"The 'wall of separation between church and state' is a metaphor based on bad history, a metaphor which has proved useless as a guide to judging. It should be frankly and explicitly abandoned."

-Chief Justice William Rehnquist

Those are fairly serious words coming from a fairly powerful man! And several of the recent appointees to the Supreme Court have rather conservative leanings as well. But the image of the beast involves apostate Protestantism

in America. Right now as you read there are millions of
well-meaning Christians who would love to see the wall of
separation come down.

Pat Robertson's Christian Coalition, for instance, claims
325 local chapters in 42 states, with over 700,000 members.
Robertson has tremendous political leverage. Certain
candidates for public office stand to lose his broad base of
voter-support if their stance on a particular issue is not in
line with his agenda. He is adamantly against the separation
of church and state, as are his followers. And he favors
mandatory Sunday rest laws, many of which are still on the
books of our cities and states.

The Religious Right in the United States is a growing
force with lobbyists stationed at our nation's state and
federal legislatures. There is a movement in American
Protestantism to "get back to God" and the Judeo-Christian
foundations our country was built upon. This is due to the
liberal trends of our society and the moral declension that is
so prevalent. But it is generally forgotten that our country
has historically protected the rights of individual conscience.

Although I rejoice at the many conversions taking place
daily, I must say that the thought of well-meaning but
intolerant Christians seeking to remove our liberty of
conscience is frightening. Yet God's Word foretells it, and
He doesn't lie.

There will come a time when we will be faced with
economic hardship that will make our current problems
seem docile. At that time, we will hear the same message
heralded from our Congressional halls that is proclaimed
from our pulpits. Our tumultuous times will be blamed on
our waywardness from God as a nation, and our desecration
of His holy day. There will be a vast movement to bring

America back to the God of our forefathers. Laws will be passed to create a mandatory day of rest: Sunday. It will be said that this is a token of our collective desire to return the control of our nation to God, in whom we trust.

I love my country. I currently serve in the United States Army Reserve as a Chaplain Candidate. I am deeply grateful to all the brave men and women who have given their lives in order to defend the freedoms I enjoy. No matter what anyone says around the world, I am still proud to be an American. We have our share of problems. But there is absolutely no place in the world like the U.S.A. No nation has enjoyed so much liberty; and no nation has had the guts to defend it like we have.

But when they tell me that I must give up my allegiance to God and His holy seventh-day Sabbath, and observe a day which the devil himself has promoted throughout history, I'll have to say, **"No! I'm sorry. The Lord Jesus who died for me is the Lord of the Sabbath! We ought to obey God rather than men!"** (Matthew 12:8; Acts 5:29).

Oh, America, America! My beloved country. If you only knew what dreadful role you will play in these final days. Oh, my friend, listen deeply to the Spirit's voice. He is calling you into the Light of Truth. He is calling you into full disciplehood. Will you follow?

Chapter 13

OLD LIES IN A NEW AGE

I t was an unusually hot spring day in 1990—not at all the kind of day preferable for transporting oneself through city traffic. But of necessity I was. In my thoughts was a stream of recent occurrences: a young UC Berkeley girl who had been abducted and murdered; violence once more in South Africa; Lithuania's freedom pangs virtually squelched; and a Community Services director who was shot to death in front of her Oakland home.

Having activated my car stereo's scan feature, I quickly stopped it on a station where it seemed solutions were being offered. The bright, positive words were those of a young woman: "Remember today, as you gaze within at the truly wonderful person you are, that nothing can go wrong. You are perfect. Everything in the world is perfect. Try to discover your eternal Self this day, and celebrate your oneness with all that is around you."

It was spiritually sickening, and I had to fight back the sarcastic laughter, though some of it escaped. I turned the stereo off and inwardly thanked God for allowing His Son to die for an imperfect me, and for the fact that by His grace I was NOT one with all that was around me.

The only thing "new" about the New Age Movement is its packaging. The contents are nearly 6,000 years old.

Lies—pure lies—are every bit as glamorous today as they were in the Garden of Eden; and every bit as deadly as well. Which lies? I refer you to Genesis chapter three. Here we find Satan calling God a liar. After Eve explains to the Serpent that departure from the will of God will naturally result in death, Satan responds by flatly saying, "You will NOT surely die. For God knows that when you eat of it your eyes will be opened, and you will be like God, knowing good and evil" (verses 4 and 5).

A simple piece of fruit, and yet a sin most devastating. For it was during those moments that the human race was separated from a Father of love; and only the blood of God Himself could win us back. Lie number one was that sin does not result in the eternal death of the sinner. Lie number two was that, having once sinned, we would "be like God."

The New Age Movement, which began in the 1960's and whose basic tenets of belief can be traced directly to Eastern religion, utilizes these two lies today. Lie number one, in apostate Christianity, translates to the unbiblical teaching of the immortality of the soul, which we will discuss in our next section. In the New Age Movement it translates to the teaching of reincarnation.

Lie number two in both instances translates to the doctrine of pantheism, which teaches that all the forces, laws, and members of the universe, animate and inanimate, are ONE with God—that God is IN everything. Thus, a major thrust of New Agers is the pursuit and development of one's "God consciousness," or "universal consciousness," or "world soul" (Hinduism), or "divine mind" (Christian Science). Whatever the terminology, the source is the Serpent's mouth.

Although you will rarely find the word "pantheism" in New Age literature, the terms used by writers presenting the New Age worldview merely mask this unbiblical teaching. However, a word you will come across often is "energy." In the New Age sense, "energy" is that reality which undergirds all nature. Energy is something that can be manipulated, when one activates one's "higher powers." In the New Age Movement there is a subjective emphasis on these powers, or one's "God-Self." Adherents look WITHIN for the source of insight and healing, rather than looking to an external, transcendent God and to objective guidelines that exist outside oneself.

The Word of God plainly teaches that solutions should be seen not in terms of SELF, but rather in terms of the SUPPLANTING of self with CHRIST. Jesus said, "If anyone would come after me, he must *deny himself* and take up his cross and follow me" (Matthew 16:24). It has always been the purpose of Satan to lead people to rely on their own inclinations instead of on God and His wisdom and will. In fact, it was the Serpent who led Eve to believe there was some *higher* attainment of knowledge *beyond* the expressed will of God to humankind. Solutions are not found by uplifting SELF. That itself is the central problem of humanity.

The New Age is the age that challenges us to use *our power* to *create* whatever happiness we need in our lives. One's pains are seen as manifestations of emotional glitches, which in turn are caused by our *thoughts*. This is where meditation comes in to the picture. In Transcendental Meditation (TM), the individual seeks to rise above the level of conscious thoughts, entering an altered state of consciousness. It's called "transcendental" because sensory perception is transcended—it actually is shut down with the repetition of a word or mantra (chant), or sometimes with deep silence. The conceptual activity of the mind ceases as the brain shifts gears to neutral. This passive state, David

Haddon notes, "resembles that sought by mediums in order to make contact with spirits. . . ."*

Shirley MacLaine says when she meditates she listens to soft music and tries to allow her mind to have "no thoughts at all."** I'm sure the devil appreciates Ms. MacLaine's best-sellers telling people to have "no thoughts at all," for the mind with no thoughts is just the kind of mind he loves to control. No wonder the Lord admonishes us, "Do not conform any longer to the pattern of this world, but be transformed by the renewing of your mind. Then you will be able to test and approve what God's will is—his good, pleasing and perfect will" (Romans 12:2).

In the New Age, the created becomes the Creator. This idea was concocted by Lucifer himself in heaven. Far different from this is the experience of the Christian, who would never indulge in such self-centered thinking, but would adhere to the counsel of the apostle: "We demolish arguments and every pretension that sets itself up against the knowledge of God, and we take captive every thought to make it obedient to Christ" (2 Corinthians 10:5).

What Happens When You Die?

There is a common belief that each person has an im-mortal soul that continues to live after we die. It is taught that it either goes to heaven or hell at that time. Perhaps you were brought up, like me, believing that deceased loved-ones were in heaven looking down at you. What if I told you

---

* David Haddon, "Transcendental Meditation Wants You," *Eternity* (November 1974), pp. 24-25.

** Shirley MacLaine, *Going Within: A Guide for Inner Transformation* (New York, NY: Bantam Books, 1990), page 58.

that the doctrine of the immortality of the soul was created by the devil in Eden? What if I told you that this was a pagan teaching that Catholicism adapted and Protestantism inherited?

According to the Bible, a "soul" is not something we *have;* it is something we *are.* "And the Lord God formed man of the dust of the ground, and breathed into his nostrils the breath of life; and man *became a living soul"* (Genesis 2:7, KJV). This truth can be expressed in equation form:

dust of ground + breath of God = soul

These are the two elements that comprise a living soul, or "being." If you take away either of these two things, you cease to have a soul. You cease to have a human being. Where do the dust of the ground and the breath of God go when a person dies? The Bible answers this question. "The dust returns to the ground it came from, and the spirit returns to God who gave it" (Ecclesiastes 12:7). We know that "spirit" here is the same as God's breath of life (Job 27:3; Psalm 104:29). In fact, in the original Hebrew the word translated "spirit" is "ruach" which means "wind." On the other hand, the Hebrew word for "soul" is "nephesh" which means "being."

What can we conclude so far? That at death a person's body returns to dust, the spirit or breath returns to God, and the living soul ceases to be. This is why there is a need for a resurrection of the dead at the Second Coming of Christ.

Is the Bible consistent with itself? Let's find out. According to God's Word, how much do the dead know? "For the living know that they will die, but the **dead know nothing"** (Ecclesiastes 9:5). **How many plans do they have?** "When their spirit departs, they return to the ground; on that very day **their plans come to nothing"** (Psalm 146:4). **Do they praise the Lord up in heaven?** "The **dead do not praise the Lord,** nor any who go down into silence" (Psalm 115:17, NKJV). **Do they even remember God? "No one remembers you when he is dead.** Who praises you from the grave?" (Psalm 6:5).

The Bible informs us that David, a man after God's own heart, did not go to heaven when he died. He is still waiting for the resurrection (Acts 2:29, 34). The apostle Paul, too, looked forward to the day when he would receive his reward of eternal life, at the Second Coming of Jesus Christ (2 Timothy 4:7, 8). Jesus Himself proclaims, "Behold, I am coming soon! **My reward is with me"** (Revelation 22:12). If His reward is with Him, then how can people receive their reward before He returns the second time? How can they be both in heaven and in the grave at the same time?

The Bible uses the word "soul" 1600 times, but never once says *"immortal* soul." The Bible also calls death a "sleep" 53 times. Jesus was quite consistent with Biblical teaching when He said, "Our friend Lazarus has fallen asleep; but I am going there to wake him up" (John 11:11). When His disciples were a bit confused, He further clarified, "Lazarus is dead" (verse 14).

We are told exactly what happens at the Second Advent of Jesus Christ: "For the Lord himself will come down from heaven, with a loud command, with the voice of the archangel and with the trumpet call of God, and the dead in Christ will rise first. After that, we who are still alive and are left will be caught up with them in the clouds to meet the Lord in the air. And so we will be with the Lord forever" (1 Thessalonians 4:16, 17).

According to this passage of Scripture, here is the order of events at the Second Coming:

1. The Lord Jesus descends into our atmosphere, but does not touch the ground.

2. There is a loud command, the voice of the archangel, and the trumpet call of God. (Nothing "secret" about this rapture).

3. The dead in Christ rise out of their graves.

4. Those who are alive in Christ then rise to meet them and the Lord in the clouds.

Even Martin Luther believed that the dead are asleep in the grave, and come back to life in the resurrection. Referring to the words of Solomon in Ecclesiastes, that the dead know nothing, the Reformer says:

"There is, saith he, no duty, no science, no knowledge, no wisdom there. Solomon judgeth that the dead are asleep, and feel nothing at all. For the dead lie there, accounting neither days nor years, but when they are awaked, they shall seem to have slept scarce one minute." -*Exposition of Solomon's Booke Called Ecclesiastes*, p. 152.

The Truth Shall Protect You

The Bible tells us that people in the last days will miss out on eternity because they refuse to cherish the truth that God holds out to them. "They perish because they refused to love the truth and so be saved" (2 Thessalonians 2:10). The truth contained in the Word of God acts as a barrier of protection in our lives, because "Your enemy the devil prowls around like a roaring lion looking for someone to devour" (2 Peter 5:8). Remember that the very first lie the Father of Lies uttered was "You will *not* surely die" (Genesis 3:4).

The doctrine of man's consciousness in death has prepared the way for modern spiritualism. Many believe that the spirits of the dead can return to converse with them. They attempt to make contact with deceased relatives in seances. Others seek the help of New Age channelers, who supposedly make contact with spirits and offer their bodies to them as temporary mediums through which to communicate to the living. Let it be known that those who entertain these spirits are entertaining "deceiving spirits and things taught by demons" (1 Timothy 4:1).

These people are giving company to Satan and his demons and they don't even know it! There is absolutely no way that Uncle Fred or Grandmother Louise can appear in your house when they have been dead for years. If you see something, it is a demon *disguised* as Uncle Fred or Grandmother Louise.

Don't be fooled. God's truth will protect you. Believe the Bible when it says that they are sleeping peacefully in the grave. Take comfort in the fact that the very next thing they will see is the glorious appearing of their Lord and Savior Jesus Christ.

Chapter 14

THE RIGHT ATTITUDE

I n the beginning God created. . . ." (Genesis 1:1). "The earth is the Lord's, and everything in it, the world, and all who live in it" (Psalm 24:1). GOD IS OWNER! It is the inescapable conclusion the reader of the Bible comes to. He owns everything. He owns you and me. In fact, He owns us *twice:* by Creation, and by Redemption. Every possession we hold so dear to our hearts has been SHARED with us by our heavenly Father. And so we are *stewards* of life.

What is a steward? A steward is someone who is entrusted with the management of another's property and resources. Stewardship, then, for the Christian, is managing the property and resources that God has shared with us efficiently and in such a way that glory is brought to Him. Stewardship involves one's WHOLE LIFE, since ALL of us belongs to Him. Whole-life stewardship is the Christian's only appropriate response to the God who gives. Let's break it down.

My Body, His Temple

"Do you not know that your body is a temple of the Holy Spirit, who is in you, whom you have received from God? You are not your own; you were bought at a price. Therefore honor God with your body" (1 Corinthians 6:19,

20). The disciple should stay away from anything that would harm the body in any way. We are walking temples of the living God! This recognition should keep us from indulging in that which destroys or harms our bodies or our minds.

Temperance goes with Christianity like strawberry jam goes with peanut butter. Just the thought makes me hungry. God has given us the blessings of sunlight, exercise, fresh air, fresh water, adequate rest, and healthy diet to promote happiness and longevity in His people. We should fill our lives with these blessings as much as possible. Health is not an option for the disciple of Christ. Health is a moral issue.

The original diet given in the Garden of Eden consisted of fruits, grains, nuts, and vegetables (see Genesis 1:29). No flesh was eaten at first. After the Flood wiped out all vegetation, God permitted His people to eat meat, but He specified which animals were "clean" and which were "unclean" (see Leviticus 11 and Deuteronomy 14). Most of the animals He prohibited them to eat were either scavengers, or animals that ate on the ocean floor or the ground.

Many of today's health problems are directly traceable to diet and lifestyle. Studies are increasingly showing that a vegetarian diet is not only adequate, but superior to a diet consisting of flesh. Vegetarians tend to live longer as well. I believe the Great Dietician knew what He was doing when He gave Adam and Eve the optimum diet. Having been raised as a meat-eater, I can testify that giving up meat has made a huge difference in my overall productivity and well-being. I *feel* better.

My Abilities, His Investment

Whether it be natural talents, developed abilities, or spiritual gifts, the Christian is to use them to advance the kingdom of God. We are not to use what the Lord has given us to glorify ourselves. This is seen so often in our world. All this talent and energy expended to promote a delicate mixture of water, clay, and a few minerals! "What is man that you are mindful of him?" (Psalm 8:4). We appear on the grand stage of earth's history for just a brief moment. And yet the Living God thinks highly and often of us, sends His beloved Son to die for us, and cares enough to walk daily with us. Out of sheer gratitude we should put our talents to use in the uplifting of humanity, with whom God so lovingly identifies.

Our Lord Jesus wants us not only to use the abilities He's given us; He wants us to *multiply* them (see Matthew 25:14-30). Some of the talents with which we have been entrusted are *dormant:* they need to be expanded and improved with hard work. Then we can present to God our very best. This is the kind of service the King requires; and it is the kind He inspires. There is no place for mediocrity in the life of a Christian. God has given His very best to us. Let's give it back.

My Time, His Agenda

There are only 24 hours in a day. I've often thought that if they insist on having a national Sunday law someday, instead of requiring rest on Sunday, they should *add* another Sunday to the week! Maybe then I could get all my work done!

If you are anything like me, you never quite catch up. There is always something else that needs to be gotten to. But when we remember that all of our time is really God's time, it helps to put things in perspective. Time is absolutely precious. Whether used efficiently or wasted, one thing is certain. *Time keeps moving!*

We must remember that GOD HAS A PLAN! At the beginning of each new day, we should pause to ask the Lord what *He* would like to accomplish through us. I believe that God makes appointments in advance for us, and it is our duty and our privilege to meet those appointments. When we lay all of our plans at the feet of Jesus Christ, we can rest assured that *His* agenda will be accomplished in our lives.

One-seventh of the week is to be set aside for holy use, because God Himself has sanctified the Sabbath. And what God has sanctified, let no man *un*sanctify. On the seventh-day, Saturday, there is a special blessing available that is not available on any other day. There really is no substitute for the true Sabbath experience. It is a time of celebrating our relationship with the Father, Son, and Holy Spirit. It is a time for standing in awe at what God has created. It is a time for family closeness after a long and hectic week. It is a time of rest. And it is a time for blessing others.

Scientists have discovered seven-day rhythms in physiology.* Apparently, our heart rates, production of steroid hormones, post-surgery swelling, and certain immune reactions all have a natural seven-day rhythm! God does not need to have a "wherefore" behind his commandments. But isn't it nice to know that our best interest is built right in to them? God understands that which He has designed.

My Money, His Blessing

All of our possessions are *shared* possessions. And all of our money—no matter how little we have—is a gift of the Lord. One way of judging character is by studying how a

---

* See Bernell Baldwin, Ph.D. "Seven-day Rhythms," *Journal of Health and Healing*, Vol 9, No 4 (1984); pp. 3, 14.

person uses his money. Being rich is not a sin. Keeping it all to yourself is. The love of money is an idol of many today. It has always been that way. It destroys spiritual health and ruins families. Since we are so prone to worship money, God made it a test.

He doesn't like competition. He knows that no other god can give us life, and so He instituted a plan whereby we can regularly show that we trust HIM for everything in life. It's called the tithe and the offering. A tithe is simply a tenth of one's increase; a tenth of one's gross income. Even though it ALL belongs to God, He only asks for ten percent to be returned. It's not because He needs our money—remember that God has a different Currency up there. Rather, returning tithes and offerings frees *us* from the entanglement of materialism.

"Will a man rob God? Yet you rob me. But you ask, 'How do we rob you?' 'In tithes and offerings. . . . Bring the whole tithe into the storehouse, that there may be food in my house. Test me in this,' says the Lord Almighty, 'and see if I will not throw open the floodgates of heaven and pour out so much blessing that you will not have room enough for it'" (Malachi 3:8, 10).

The tithe and the offering are to be used for the Lord's work in the world. And we are promised a blessing if we return these to Him. It's a matter of TRUST. GOD is the One who puts food on our tables. He is our sole Sustainer. I have never seen a tithing Christian go hungry.

My World, His Creation

"The earth is the Lord's" (Psalm 24:1). Isn't that reason enough to take care of it? We are to be stewards of this world's life and resources. We are to manage the earth, not manipulate it. The Lord has entrusted the keeping of this planet to us, and it is a shame that we cannot bring ourselves to cohabitate responsibly with the rest of God's creation.

The fact that we are stewards of the earth has tremendous implications. It means that we can no longer toss a piece of garbage out of our car window while driving. Even if there were no law against it, we are still sinning against the OWNER of the environment. The fact that we are stewards means that we must stop the wholesale, irresponsible pollution of our atmosphere. It means that we must find cleaner, more efficient fuels that will help ensure that our children will also have an environment to enjoy.

God's warning for those who abuse His planet is serious. He says that there is coming a time when He will destroy "those who destroy the earth" (Revelation 11:18).

My Children, His Church

Yes, families are important to God. He wants to guard our families against Satan's manifold attacks. Often we forget that our children are His gifts to us, to raise in an atmosphere of peace, and in the knowledge of God. So many things compete for our time with our kids. Often the TV becomes the babysitter, or worse yet, they come home from school to an empty house. It's rough enough having to grow up nowadays. But unless we parents are there for them, our children will adopt an alternative support system that may be quite undesirable.

Our children ARE the future! They are God's Church in this world. We should remember that when raising our children we are raising up the leadership base of this world. Godly homes make Godly neighborhoods, which make Godly societies, which make Godly nations. If a Christian places his family high on his list of priorities, the world can be changed for the good.

Chapter 15

STEPPING OUT IN FAITH

Y our reading of this book has been no mistake. God made this appointment with you long ago, to meet with you and speak to your heart in such a way that you would be drawn to Him. I hope you have been.

His plan for you includes full membership in His family through the shed blood of Jesus Christ, His Son. Salvation is offered to you freely. Just take it.

His plan for you includes a daily connection with Jesus, through the reading of His Word and through prayer, so you can learn to walk as His disciple.

His plan for you includes a complete set of spiritual armor, so you can take your stand against the devil. And He promises to send His angels to watch over you and your household.

His plan for you includes the discovery of ABUNDANT MEANING and FULFILLMENT in life, through your exercise of the spiritual gift(s) He has given to you, and your participation in a local church.

His plan for you includes your acceptance of Jesus Christ as heavenly High Priest; your Defense Attorney as well as your Judge during this time of judgment.

His plan for you includes the privilege of resting on God's holy seventh-day Sabbath, and all attendant blessings. His Word testifies to this truth, and to the significant role the Sabbath will play in these final days.

His plan for you includes an awareness of Satan's inroads into apostate Christianity, including the false doctrine of the immortality of the soul.

His plan for you includes your role as steward. Everything in life is a gift that has been entrusted to you. Thus, a new attitude of faithful management of life takes over, and temperance becomes a moral issue.

There is only one church in the entire world that teaches all of these aspects of God's plan for your life. It is the Seventh-day Adventist Church. It is the church of which I am a member. It is the only fellowship that has passed the scrutiny of God's Word. Though we are not perfect, we uphold the eternal truth of the Bible, against the opposition of long-standing tradition.

Adventists are a people of destiny. For instance, the book of Daniel was a "sealed" book (Daniel 8:26). It was meant for the "distant future." That is why it did not begin to be fully understood until the mid-1800's, when William Miller, a Baptist preacher, started studying his Bible carefully. It was discovered that the books of Daniel and Revelation cover much of the same ground. A scattered group of devout Christians from various churches searched the Scriptures, and there they discovered the heavenly Sanctuary, the Sabbath, and many other neglected doctrines.

They formed the Seventh-day Adventist Church—a movement to proclaim Christ's soon Second Advent, and to draw the minds of people back to the plain Word of God. The Adventist Church is the only church that has remained faithful to the Protestant Reformation. We speak out in Christian love against all forms of apostasy, in direct fulfillment of the Three Angels' Messages of Revelation 14—God's final altar call.

My friend, I want to take this opportunity to invite you to become a member of this church that I love dearly. I believe that God is calling everyone to a full acceptance of His truth in these last days, and the honest in heart will follow. Will you step out in faith today?

If this is your desire, call the toll-free 800 number at the back of this book, or fill out the page and send it to the address indicated. We will be happy to connect you with your local Adventist pastor or Bible-worker.

Many are praying for you just now. Remember that Jesus stepped out of the heavenly courts, and came to this earth to save you by dying on a cruel cross. Can you honestly look Him in the eyes and say "No?" Can you decline His invitation of mercy? Take a stand for Jesus and His truth today.

I pray that you will not take my words, or anyone's words, for granted. You owe it to yourself to search the Scriptures to find out whether these things are true. I did. And I believe.

FREE AND WITHOUT OBLIGATION, I WOULD LIKE:

☐ To study the Bible with someone.
☐ To pray with someone.
☐ A personal visit from a Christian in my area.
☐ The book *Steps to Christ.*
☐ The book *Cosmic Conflict*, which reveals how Bible prophecy is being fulfilled in modern history.

Date: _____

Name: _____

Address: _____

City: _____ State: _____ Zip: _____

Phone: (_____) _____

I WOULD ALSO LIKE TO KNOW MORE ABOUT:

☐ Daniel and Revelation
☐ Why Adventists worship on Saturday
☐ Healthful living
☐ Communication in Marriage
☐ Single-parenting
☐ Defeating a low self-concept
☐ How to stop smoking
☐ Creation vs. Evolution
☐ What Seventh-day Adventists believe

Call 1-800-253-3000

Or mail this page to:

God's Plan For Your Life
Information Ministry
Berrien Springs, MI 49104-0970

FOR ADDITIONAL COPIES OF THIS BOOK

Send $3.50 per copy (1-10 copies), $3.25 per copy (11-20 copies), or $3.00 per copy (21 or more copies).

Send me _____ copy(ies) at $_____ per copy.
Total Enclosed _____

Name: _____
Address: _____
_____
City: _____ St: _____ Zip: _____

Make check or money order payable to David Sullivan.
Note: All monies received are used to meet printing and shipping costs. Price includes shipping and handling.
Send Orders To:
David Sullivan
550 Maplewood Ct. C-62
Berrien Springs, MI 49103

FOR ADDITIONAL COPIES OF THIS BOOK

Send $3.50 per copy (1-10 copies), $3.25 per copy (11-20 copies), or $3.00 per copy (21 or more copies).

Send me _____ copy(ies) at $_____ per copy.
Total Enclosed _____

Name: _____
Address: _____
_____
City: _____ St: _____ Zip: _____

Make check or money order payable to David Sullivan.
Note: All monies received are used to meet printing and shipping costs. Price includes shipping and handling.
Send Orders To:
David Sullivan
550 Maplewood Ct. C-62
Berrien Springs, MI 49103

DATE DUE

GAYLORD			PRINTED IN U.S.A.